Praise for *You Belong Here*

"*You Belong Here* is a totally fresh take on how to create a culture of psychological safety that liberates people to fully express their talents."

SUSAN UTHAYAKUMAR, MD, chief energy and sustainability officer, Prologis

"Mike Lipkin and Dr. Diane McIntosh have pulled off a remarkable feat. They combine brain science with practical leadership techniques to create a breakthrough guide that will change the way you live and work."

JOHN RUFFOLO, founder and managing partner, Maverix Private Equity

"*You Belong Here* expresses Mike Lipkin and Dr. Diane McIntosh's best insights in ways that are immediately actionable—especially in the current environment."

DANI REISS, CEO, Canada Goose

"*You Belong Here* is a guide to a brighter future... one built on optimism, connection, and deliberate action."

MARTIN PERELMUTER, president, Speakers Spotlight

"Many of us operate below our potential, especially when we navigate higher degrees of uncertainty, insecurity, and fear. Mike Lipkin and Dr. Diane McIntosh inspire us to empower our people by making it safe to be bold. Great and grounding read!"

SILVIO STROESCU, head, BMO Wealth Digitech Transformation, and president, BMO InvestorLine, BMO Financial Group

"You've heard of *Good to Great*? Well, consider this your Guide to Great: Great insights. Great writing. Great ideas. Great victories."

RON TITE, author of *Think. Do. Say.* and *Everyone's an Artist*

"Mike Lipkin and Dr. Diane McIntosh have written a book that expresses the core of leadership effectiveness: making it safe to be great. On top of it all, it's a highly enjoyable read."

MIKE PARRA, CEO, Europe, DHL Express

"In a world that seems to be getting more dangerous and increasingly stressful, you wonder how to complete your projects and be a leader. Start with this collaboration between Canada's coach Mike Lipkin and leading psychiatrist of depression Dr. Diane McIntosh. Their combined wisdom will show you how to feel safe to take risks and prevail in chaotic times."

MICHAEL ADAMS, chairman, Environics Research Group

"Mike Lipkin and Dr. Diane McIntosh have taken it to the next level in *You Belong Here*. I'm inspired about creating my next breakthrough moment. After reading this book, you will be too."

KAREN WERGER, CPA, CA, CBV vice chair,
Global Leader Valuations & Modeling, Deloitte LLP

"Through thought-provoking storytelling and insightful observations, this book takes readers on a journey of self-discovery."

JEFF SROUR, SVP and chief information officer,
Corporate Business Technology, Johnson & Johnson

"Mike Lipkin and Dr. Diane McIntosh highlight the power of belonging and the resulting feeling of emotional safety in unblocking people's potential. You can read this book to be a better leader; however, I'm certain reading it will help you be a better person."

ADRIAN THOMAS, CEO, Hammond Power Solutions

"In a world where technology is creating increasing isolation, *You Belong Here* warms the heart and connects the reader with a renewed sense of belonging and purpose. This is a great book for leaders who want to empower their teams to make a positive impact on the world."

KAREN BROOKMAN, president and CEO, WCD on-demand print and information solutions

"With Mike Lipkin's and Dr. Diane McIntosh's sincere encouragement and energy, the words 'You Belong Here' succinctly describe the many road signs on a fruitful journey to becoming worthy leaders. A wonderful read."

DOUG LOVSIN, president, Freson Bros.

"*You Belong Here* is a great win for readers. Every chapter of this book checked each of my boxes, covering past experiences, present knowing, and future action. I was left completely inspired to make some new moves."

KAREN AZLEN, founder and CEO, Introduction Capital

"The authors have masterfully laid out a detailed framework of why 'You Belong Here' (YBH). If a leader embraces the 7 Core Components of YBH, and utilizes them to their fullest, they will create a culture of safety and belonging, allowing people to do their best work and look out for others!"

PAUL TONET, general manager, WD-40 Company Canada

"This book was written for me and my team. The collaboration between Mike Lipkin and Dr. Diane McIntosh generously shares some of their personal and professional insights that helped me validate my own perspectives on key topics explored in the book. *You Belong Here* will be a reference for me as I continue my career and personal relationships."

JIM HUNT, vice president, sales, Palliser Furniture Upholstery Ltd.

YOU BELONG HERE

YOU BELONG

MIKE LIPKIN & DR. DIANE McINTOSH

HERE

How to Make People Feel Safe to Be Their Best, Take Bold Risks, and Win

PAGE TWO

Some names and identifying details have been changed
to protect the privacy of individuals.

This book is not intended as a substitute for the medical
advice of physicians. The reader should regularly consult
a physician in matters relating to their health and particularly
with respect to any symptoms that may require diagnosis
or medical attention.

Cataloguing in publication information is available from
Library and Archives Canada.
ISBN 978-1-77458-428-6 (paperback)
ISBN 978-1-77458-429-3 (ebook)

Page Two
pagetwo.com

Edited by James Harbeck
Copyedited by Indu Singh
Proofread by Rachel Ironstone
Cover and interior design by Cameron McKague
Brain illustration by Jeff Winocur
Printed and bound in Canada by Friesens

mikelipkin.com
drdianemcintosh.com

To the Gods of Serendipity and the People of Canada—
you made this book possible.

MIKE LIPKIN

To my brilliant, brave, and compassionate RAPIDS *teammates who, through brain massages, Frankenstein-ing, and remarkable trust, always helped me find the best path ahead.*

DR. DIANE McINTOSH

Contents

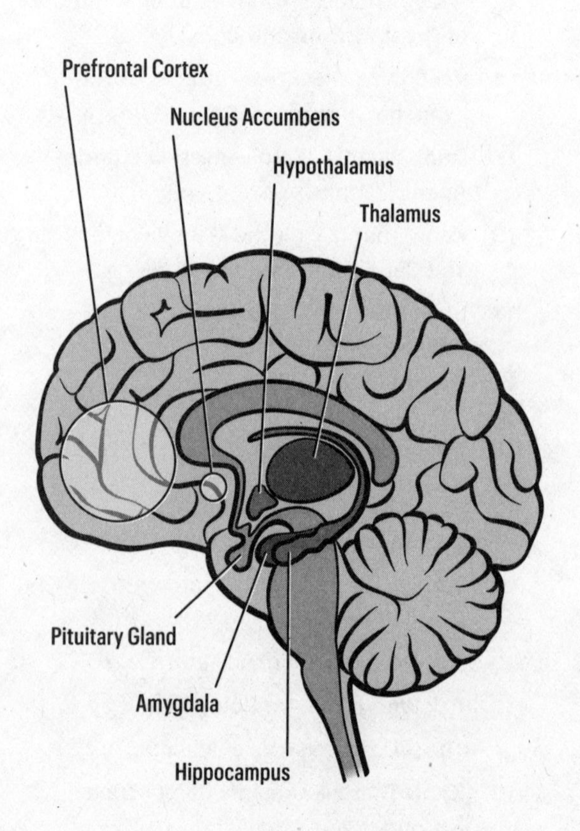
Prefrontal Cortex
Nucleus Accumbens
Hypothalamus
Thalamus
Pituitary Gland
Amygdala
Hippocampus

Introduction

"ARE YOU a psychopath?"

That's the first thing Diane asked me when I proposed the idea of writing this book with her.

"Whaaat? Are you kidding me?" I responded. In my thirty-year career, I had never been asked that question. I didn't even know what a psychopath was. I just knew it was something awful—someone who lacked a conscience or compassion—the stuff that serial killers were made of. But I was only mildly shocked by the question because Diane is known for her unconventional style and uncompromising candour. She was also smiling as she observed my bemused expression.

"A psychopath is someone who lacks empathy. They're often superficially charming, but they're morally vacuous, impulsive, insensitive to the needs of others, and they don't care about the impacts of their own actions, including punishment," Diane explained. "And believe it or not, they comprise about 12 percent of corporate leadership." She also made me take a psychopathy test that required me to rate myself on statements such as:

- Most would describe me as charming and nonchalant—I can turn my charm on and off like a faucet.
- I do what I want, when I want, the moment the impulse strikes me, regardless of what others want.
- If something goes wrong or turns out badly, it's not my fault.
- Every person for themselves; I don't see the point in feeling sorry for other people and have no desire to help others.
- I have no problem or concern in lying in order to get what I want.

I was relieved to report that my scores showed I was the opposite of a psychopath. In fact, I care way too much about the feelings of others. I second-guess whatever I say because I'm afraid to offend or disturb people. I'm compelled to please, even to my detriment. Like most people, I need to feel like I'm connecting with people, not alienating them. My desire for approval feeds my need for social belonging—even with people I've just met. As a professional nomad who makes a living by literally going from company to company coaching their team members, I need to establish an immediate rapport with each organization. Even though I'm an outsider, I need to feel part of the groups I'm with, even if it's only for a short while.

Diane's reason for asking the question was that, in her multiple roles as psychiatrist, businessperson, and entrepreneur, she has worked with a few people who turned out to be psychopaths. It was always a deeply disturbing experience. Above all, she wanted to feel safe with me as her partner in this literary venture.

"Is it safe?" is the fundamental question we ask ourselves, often unconsciously, before we engage in any activity—or at least we should. While we may hold differing definitions of safety, most adults want to protect themselves from danger, hurt, or loss. Even those people who consider themselves risk-takers (like Diane and me) also consider themselves disciplined planners—or they seek advice from knowledgeable consultants. Except for the most reckless people, risk aversion or mitigation is a key shaper of our mindsets in every aspect of life—financial, social, and physical.

You must feel safe in order to feel you belong, so the twin themes of belonging and safety will permeate the pages ahead. There is safety in numbers, especially when you're with people you like and trust. Belonging brings its own kind of security and stability. It promotes a sense of personal well-being and a desire to play at one's best and do what's best for the team. On the other hand, being compelled to spend time with people you don't like or trust is its own special kind of hell. At some point in our careers, we may have to endure this affliction, but our sanity depends on getting out of it fast.

The safety that we discuss in this book is not the false safety of inertia, which comes from staying in your comfort zone. It's the safety that comes from belonging, which gives you license to take risks and be your best, secure in the knowledge that you'll be rewarded for your courage. If you're a leader, you're accountable for creating this kind of culture—where people are encouraged to stretch their capacity and swing for the fences, even if they strike out. As Thomas J. Watson, former CEO of IBM, said, "If you want to increase your success rate, double your failure rate."

Paradoxically, belonging and safety create the willingness to take bold risks and win. In its July 21, 2023, issue,

Newsweek asked some probing questions on this subject and came to the following conclusions: "What happens when a company pays its employees fairly... promotes equality and diversity and cultivates a culture open to new ideas? What if it also provides a comfortable environment while encouraging career development and work-life balance? These key employee satisfaction touchpoints foster a sense of belonging and optimism. Employees at these companies like their work and people who like what they do are more motivated and engaged... Experts say employees who like their work are more productive, and these employees have lower turnover rates. By staying at companies longer, loyal employees contribute to organizational stability and consistency. Ultimately, this enhances the bottom line."

A Unique and Unlikely Partnership with a Purpose

I met Diane for the first time in August 2018. Along with eight other leading psychiatrists, she was a member of a focus group that I conducted for a leading pharmaceutical company. As someone who has suffered from clinical depression, I was more used to being a patient than a facilitator. Yet there I was—orchestrating a conversation on the future of psychiatry in Canada with the professionals who could make it real.

Diane was the only female psychiatrist in the group. She was also the most vocal. In what I later learned was her signature style, she displayed curiosity and authority in equal measure. She alternated between challenging and supporting me throughout the five-hour conversation. In the late afternoon, when people's attention began to flag, Diane became even more engaged. That's when I knew I wanted to write a book with her.

At the time, Diane was completing her landmark book on understanding depression. In classic Diane directness, she called it *This Is Depression*. As someone who is deeply familiar with the disorder, I found it both enlightening and cathartic. She blends humanity and humour with evidence and anecdotes to create a remarkably accessible read. If you or someone you love is battling depression, this is the one guide that will help you through the darkness.

This Is Depression was published in 2019. Shortly after that, Diane assumed the role of chief neuroscience officer at Telus, a leading Canadian telecommunications company. In that position, Diane played a leading role in developing and supporting Telus' mental health business going into the pandemic. The pandemic proved her prescience, as demand for remote care exploded, which was how she'd approached her clinical practice for several years.

In 2021, with generous support from Telus and a committed team of professionals, Diane launched her own start-up called RAPIDS—an innovative technology designed to provide psychiatric guidance to clinicians and improve the quality and accessibility of psychiatric care. As a side hustle, she also launched an award-winning podcast called *Blindsided* together with ex-NHL goaltender Corey Hirsch. It explores the impact of mental illness through the experiences of professional athletes, showing that mental health struggles know no economic or demographic bounds and do not discriminate based on apparent privilege. I will warn you that it is a searing series of stories that will shake you to your core before it lifts you up again.

In June 2022, I connected with Diane again and proposed the idea of this book to her. After I passed the psychopathy test, she enthusiastically embraced the project. Our skill sets complement each other perfectly. I'm the motivator, marketer, and trend spotter. Diane is the scientist, academic, mental health activist, and medical professional. We also share a robust irreverence for the status quo and a love of learning—while laughing. We both seem oddly fascinated with the other, perhaps because we process and share ideas in our own, mutually idiosyncratic manner, so we both approached our weekly virtual conversations with excited anticipation.

Inertia Is Not an Option—and Neither Is Indifference

Most importantly, Diane and I are out to make a positive impact on the world. For us, inertia is not an option—and neither is indifference. The ideas, insights, prompts, and provocations we put forward in the following pages are designed to spur you into action.

At a time when people feel more alone and alienated than ever, perhaps the most valuable thing you can do is help others to feel like they belong. If you can help someone feel like they're connected, valued, supported, loved, trusted, and capable of greatness, they will reciprocate, royally. In fact, one person can be a community to another person. Most of us remember a person who was there for us when we really needed them. That person might have appeared at just the right time to welcome us into a new environment, shepherded us through a difficulty, inspired us as we faced a new challenge, guided us through a crisis, or restored our faith after a setback. They helped to build the bridge between who we were and who we wanted or needed to be. They restored our belief in the goodness of others.

Canadian soccer legend and Olympic gold medallist Christine Sinclair said, "We're not going to be the best until everyone feels like they belong, so that's the type of leader I try to be."

That's our mission: to guide you to be a leader that makes people feel like they belong so they realize their full potential, become their best self, and pay it forward, helping others to do the same. In our book, a leader doesn't mean someone with command and control over others. It means someone who influences and enhances the lives of others by example. In other words, someone like you.

As you continue to read, you'll notice that, despite being a book about belonging, we often highlight the importance of mental health. That's because your success at work, success as a leader, and success in life are highly influenced by your mental health. And if it's suboptimal, you won't function at the level that allows you, and those you support, to prosper.

Like many aspects of our lives, mental health exists on a spectrum. While many of us consider ourselves mentally healthy, we all have times when we feel highly stressed or under pressure, whether at work, school, or home. Sometimes that stress keeps us from performing optimally at work or from being the partner, parent, friend, or colleague we know we can or should be. Sometimes a constellation of factors can lead to a severe mental health problem, such as clinical depression. We want to share insights you can use to address challenges, wherever you are on the mental health spectrum, to keep you healthy or move you back toward optimal mental health.

There is never one reason why someone develops a mental illness like depression. There are many factors, including genetics, brain chemicals, such as hormones and neurotransmitters, our childhood experiences, and our current environment. While all are important, Diane believes that strong social support is one of the greatest protectors of mental health—and scientific research backs her up.

Your mental health is a function of the environment in which you live. You become the company you keep. Healthy, happy people create healthy, happy communities. If you feel like you belong where you are, you're motivated to give more of yourself. You feel safe to open up and reveal more of yourself. You're willing to risk more of yourself on behalf of your stakeholders because you know they've got your back. Even when you experience moments of conflict, you know they're temporary because of people's commitment to each other. Based on our combined research and experience, Diane and I believe that a sense of belonging, together with the feeling of safety that comes with it, is essential for a person's overall feeling of well-being and empowerment. One is not only the loneliest number, it's also the least effective.

Conversely, experiencing poor mental health is by its nature isolating. When someone is severely depressed, they often feel utterly useless, worthless, and hopeless. How can you feel like you belong when your brain is telling you such cruel lies? Knowing you belong comes with a sense of value, worth, and hope. If your mental health is not at its best, you won't feel like you belong and you won't be able to help others to feel like they belong.

Where We're Going and How We'll Get There

As you can see, this book is written in the first person. I'm narrating the combined insights that emerged from the dozens of conversations between Diane and me, from June 2022 to July 2023. Everything you read in the following pages is a fusion of our collective effort. The book has five parts:

1. **Creating Belonging in a Hybrid World:** We'll begin by exploring what it means to create a sense of belonging through our language, mindsets, and behaviours, especially in a hybrid (in-person and virtual) environment.

2. **Growing Enriching Relationships:** Then we'll share how to grow relationships that foster engagement and connection while they enrich everyone involved.

3. **Owning Your Power:** We'll then introduce you to the great psychological paradox: you become more like the people with whom you spend the most time, but the only person you can control is you. You'll learn about your remarkable capacity for change, how to reprogram your brain, and how to reassess your past so it supercharges your future.

4. **Winning on the Brink:** Then we'll explain why you must take yourself to the brink of burnout in order to create breakthroughs with others. We'll also coach you on how to prevent yourself from going over the edge while you help others down from the ledge.

5. **Showing the Way:** We'll then share how you can intentionally become an icon of resilience, integrity, and safety who inspires others to achieve similar status—resilience is something you can learn, build, and share. And we'll give you a simple blueprint for creating a future that ensures the best days are always ahead.

I

Creating Belonging in a Hybrid World

III

Owning Your Power

II

Growing Enriching Relationships

Winning on the Brink

V

Showing the Way

PART I

CREATING BELONGING IN A HYBRID WORLD

1

Speak the Language of "You Belong Here"

YOU BELONG HERE.

Of all the compliments you can pay someone, "You belong here" may be among the greatest—especially if the place or situation is integral to the other person's well-being. The greater your authority or status in the eyes of others, the more meaningful the phrase becomes. It evokes an instant response of delight and gratitude. It also stimulates curiosity regarding your reasons for saying it.

Recently, I facilitated a three-day conference for an organization called Bluum, a large company that provides technology solutions to schools throughout North America. After the first day, one of the senior attendees approached me and said, "You belong here. You talk and sound like one of us.

I can see why you were hired." That's all I needed to hear to be even more confident for the remaining two days.

Belong may be the most emotive verb in the English language. It's both the cause and effect of happiness, love, belief, and the realization of one's dreams. It's essential for feelings of safety, comfort, and joy. It refers to time, place, culture, relationship, and mindset. It's the difference between laying down roots and looking for somewhere else to go. Its absence condemns one to a life of fear, suspicion, and isolation. It's an essential aspect of the human experience.

We're living in a peri-pandemic environment that is rife with alienation. As a leader, no matter what your job title is, your role is to make others feel like they belong. Until someone feels connected by a common bond or purpose, they won't feel safe. They'll be afraid of messing up and being embarrassed or humiliated, and all of their energy will go into preventing that from happening. It's only when they feel part of the clan that they'll be able to fully express their gifts and maximize their contribution. A single sentence or gesture can free people up to be great or constrain them, so they become defensive in order to protect themselves.

What does *belong* mean to you? Here are some of the things it can express:

- To be a member of a club, organization, or set
- To be attached or bound by birth, allegiance, or dependency
- To have the right personal or social qualities to be a member of a particular group
- To be happy and comfortable in a place or a situation
- To have the same interests, values, and ideas as other people

- To own something, have a right to it, or be responsible for it
- To feel an obligation or commitment to someone or something
- To be included or embraced by a group or organization

Belonging is a language all of its own. If you speak to people in a way that makes them feel they belong, they will be drawn to you because you never make them feel "less than" or "other," only "equal to." You'll never speak down to them, only up to them. You'll be a walking safe space in a world that can feel increasingly threatening. Most importantly, every word will reinvest you with a sense of connection to those around you. Even when you're having a difficult conversation, it will be one that is characterized by respect, compassion, and acceptance for the other person.

The language of "You Belong Here" (YBH) is the vocabulary of connection. It's a direct route to rapport and interpersonal harmony. It removes others' doubt that you don't care or you don't understand them. It's an immediate bridge to the next level in the relationship because it builds trust—others shed their fears and relax into the experience of being with you. That growing trust will ultimately create safety—not the kind of safety that boxes us into inertia, but the kind that frees us to take risks, get the creative juices flowing, and explore new ideas. Inertia is an anathema to innovation, while belonging revolutionizes.

Nothing tastes as awful as rejection, real or perceived. Nothing feels as awkward as nonacceptance by the group that you're currently with. Being ostracized by the tribe is an innate fear. In a peri-pandemic reality, many people are still nervous to venture out into the world. Their physical interactions may be less frequent than they were pre-pandemic.

Social skills, especially for younger people, may not be as well developed. Their guard is more likely to be up. They are less likely to be the ones reaching out to you. In this environment, the language of YBH becomes even more compelling because it is received with relief and reassurance.

There is a caveat to using this language—you must mean it. The affirmation it expresses must be genuine. If it doesn't come from the heart, it will alienate others. Your tone is as important as your content. Don't even try to speak YBH if you don't believe it.

The good news is that you tend to find what you're looking for. It's called "positive bias." The mere fact that you're communicating with someone means that there is a reason for your interaction. Unless the chemistry is awful, or the other person clearly stands for values that conflict with your own, you can identify qualities that uniquely qualify them to be there.

The 5 Levels of Belonging

Diane and I have identified five levels of belonging that are generalizable to every social situation or setting—including organizations. These are states that can characterize someone's experience at any given moment, and they can ebb and flow depending on how they perceive others' attitude toward them. These states are dynamic, depending on changes in circumstances or people. Think about your experiences as you review them with the ultimate prize in mind: the kind of safety that makes people free to take risks and be their best, not the kind that boxes them into inertia.

Level 1—Unwelcome: You feel like you're an intruder and you've stumbled into hostile territory. You feel unwelcome, threatened, or under attack. You may find yourself somewhere you *have* to be, not where you *want* to be. In fact, you wish you were anywhere but where you are. It may be in a room filled with adversaries or with a leader who is being confrontational, or where your proposal or offering is being torpedoed by the group. Hostility can also be expressed in subtle ways through thinly veiled comments that betray others' contempt or dismissal of you. The ability to diffuse hostility, wherever and whenever you see it forming, is an invaluable life skill. It's particularly critical in our peri-pandemic world, where hybrid workstyles can allow frustrations to go unaddressed, fomenting discontent and interpersonal conflict.

Level 2—Discomfort: You're not quite sure how to feel. Your discomfort might be caused by a clash of styles or culture. It's also when you're not confident in your knowledge or your command of the situation. You're afflicted with an inner confusion about what to think or what to do next. You experience tension because you don't know if it's you that's the problem, or them. It takes real-time self-reflection not to flee, but to stay the course and resolve your uncertainty. Ideally, someone will sense your ennui and speak the language of YBH to lift you up onto higher ground. The critical combination of your perseverance and their proactive empathy and generosity could be the difference between a terrible experience and a terrific one.

Level 3—Tolerance: You feel neither fear nor encouragement. You're not accepted but you're not rejected either. You feel ambivalent because others' response to you is ambiguous, thus you're not engaged. People are cordial to you, but they keep their distance so you still feel like you "come from away."

Their expressions of emotion feel superficial or scripted, like a faux friendliness. Your experience isn't memorable, it's mediocre. It's not accretive to your well-being.

Level 4—Acceptance: You feel comfortable and aligned with the situation. You feel encouraged to contribute more. You're engaging. You like the people around you because you feel that they like and accept you. There is a level of trust that motivates you to say more and do more. You don't feel judged or pigeonholed by your style or background. You feel safe, but to a point. You're willing to take moderate risks but not ones that take you to the brink.

Level 5—Belonging: You feel fully engaged and connected. You believe that others have totally got your back. You share a common purpose. You trust them completely. You're willing to do whatever it takes to achieve the collective goal. Collaboration is instinctive. You feel a sense of pride in being part of the organization or community. You love the people with whom you live, work, or play. You feel like you can fully express your personality. You approach each moment with enthusiasm, appreciation, and gratitude.

In every interaction, your mission should be to move people to the level of belonging. A simple greeting or a single conversation can help transport people through the levels. A well-placed phrase, a thoughtful question, or a supportive gesture can elevate them all the way. It may just be for a moment, or it may be for keeps, but your words can make the difference. Whether it's the kindness of strangers or the deep responsibility of an elected leader, it's exactly what empowers someone to believe in the goodness of others.

Think about the last time someone made your day by surprising you with a kind word or thoughtful gesture. Or, think about someone who has always been there for you when you needed them most. Was there someone whose words inspired you to grasp the prize that otherwise would have been out of your reach? You would not be reading these words without the people who empowered you to get here—including Diane and me, by the way. No matter who you are or where you are, we feel a sense of connection to you. You're signing up to a global community that is out to change the world, one sentence at a time.

THE QUICK WIN

Diane has learned that when she's feeling anxious or uneasy, simply acknowledging her feelings can be a critical step in getting herself to feel more at ease. "When I'm really worried about something, telling myself, 'This is really awful, but I always get through it... it always passes...' actually starts my journey through it and up the other side."

Think of five people whom you can reach out to and make them feel like they belong. They can be colleagues, clients, or community members. They may be new to your organization or even new to your country. What could you say to them that will stoke their sense of belonging? How could you welcome them into the fold so they feel empowered to fully express themselves?

1. **Make Others Feel Welcome**
2. **Listen with Intention**
3. **Be Cognizant of the Context of the Conversation**
4. **Be Authentic, Vulnerable, and Self-Effacing**
5. **Build Rapport by Demonstrating Your Love of Others**
6. **Declare Your Absolute Support for Others—and Follow Through**
7. **Work to Avoid Microaggressions**

THE 7 CORE COMPONENTS OF "YOU BELONG HERE"

THERE ARE SEVEN core components of speaking the language of "You Belong Here"—both verbal and non-verbal. These are specific mindsets, words, and actions that you can begin using right now to make an impact.

1. Make Others Feel Welcome

Through your expressions and gestures, show that you're glad to be with them—even when the conversation is difficult. Think about how you would express your openness, connection, or warmth. Would you smile? Would you use a gentle tone? Would your voice be loud or soft? Would your arms be open or closed? Would you appear calm or agitated? Would you seem hurried or patient?

It's easy to make others feel welcome when things are going well or when you're in a good mood. It's even easier when you have an immediate rapport or comfort with the other person. In those situations, your natural hospitality is self-evident. The time to be consciously welcoming is when you don't feel like it, or when you actively have to look for reasons to invite the other person into your circle. That's when you must remind yourself that every conversation can be a game changer in a relationship—especially if it's in its opening stages. First impressions are lasting. The first cuts are the deepest.

When I'm at an event, I look for the person who's standing by themselves. I approach them and start a conversation. If I'm a leader, I join groups of people rather than waiting for them to come to me. I introduce myself and ask questions such as:

- What's the most important thing I should know about you?
- What's the best thing that's happened to you this year?
- What are you looking forward to?
- Where did you grow up?
- What do you enjoy doing when you're not at events like these?

2. Listen with Intention

Take notice of what's being said and how it's being said. Discern the meaning behind what's being said. Be curious about others' opinions or perspectives. When Diane interviews people on her podcast, she infuses her voice with empathy, fascination, and tenderness. She consciously uses her voice as an instrument to put people at ease and open them up. She reads the room. What underlies her expression is enthusiasm. She is excited about everything her guests have to share with her, and she wants them to know it. She makes comments and asks questions that demonstrate her focus and full engagement:

- I hear you say... Is that correct?
- Let me feed this back to you so you know I've heard you...

- It sounds like you feel... Here's how we can move forward together... Does that work for you?
- It seems what's important to you in this situation is... Am I right? Can you help me understand exactly what you want so we can create the best result together?
- Is there anything I've missed? Is there anything that you would like to add? Feel free to come back to me later if you think of anything.
- I want to be a valuable resource for you. What's the best way for me to contribute to your success?
- How else can I support you so you can play at your best?
- Are you getting what you need from this relationship? Do you feel like you're being set up for success? How else can we help you win?
- I acknowledge you for what you're doing. I want to help you be even more effective by...

3. Be Cognizant of the Context of the Conversation

Know the circumstances influencing your interaction. What role does the other person play? Do they feel uncomfortable? Is the interaction addressing their needs? Is it building their sense of belonging? Do they feel safe or do they need reassurance? Are you celebrating together? What is happening in the other person's world that is impacting this interaction? How is their reality changing?

Diane isn't a hierarchical leader, so she takes a casual approach with everyone on her team. Having had no experience as a leader of a large team, especially in a system where hierarchy was engrained, meant she didn't consider that her team members viewed her as "the boss," regardless of her style. She acknowledges, "This was hard for me to learn, because I wanted to be viewed through my actions and words, not my title. However, that wasn't fair to team members who had always been used to 'they're the boss and I'm the employee.' Once I understood the dynamic, I knew I needed to build safety for my teammates for them to feel they truly belonged. And they belonged not to me, but to the team. This meant being completely engaged, respectful, and attuned to their reactions."

Ask simple questions like:

- Is this a good time for us to talk?
- How are you feeling about your role on the project?
- Are you facing any challenges I might be able to help you with?
- Do you foresee any obstacles, challenges, or quick wins ahead?
- What are the key changes that you're seeing around you?

4. Be Authentic, Vulnerable, and Self-Effacing

You must do you. But you must do the best version of yourself in any given situation. Authenticity, in the context of YBH, means you're being true to the highest expression of your character. It means that you are playing full out, not playing it safe. Ironically, playing it safe sends a signal to others that it's not safe to take risks or share one's genuine opinions.

As Diane says, "Vulnerability is a leadership superpower." If you're not afraid to be wrong or admit that you don't know, you're free to explore and discover the best outcomes, together with others. You also lift your teammates up—they see that you need and respect their opinions—and you become a role model of the desired behaviour.

No champion goes undefeated. At some point, you're going to lose. You're going to get it wrong. You will fumble, stumble, fall, and fail. Accept and embrace it. As Winston Churchill said, "In the course of my life, I have often had to eat my words, and I must confess that I have always found it a wholesome diet."

Life is too serious to treat yourself too seriously. Take your responsibility earnestly but take yourself lightly. Help people have fun by making fun of yourself before anybody else can. Appropriate self-effacement is an effective way to put others at ease. It also endears you to others by demonstrating your humility.

Diane is often the only woman in a room filled with male psychiatrists and other notables. She is sometimes mistaken for a server by her fellow guests. She doesn't protest. Instead, she'll bring them their beverage with a smile—leaving them to discover that she's the keynote speaker the following day.

Diane will also compliment her audience by stating, "I know you probably already know this . . ." or "I'm sure you're familiar with these facts . . ." or "You've probably read about this . . ." She makes sure that whomever she's speaking to knows that she respects their knowledge. It's her way of not being mistaken as arrogant or hubristic.

I will open my sessions by declaring that "I'm the best speaker you've never heard of," and "I'm someone you can count on to talk about getting it done, but never actually doing anything." I confess my continual nervousness before a talk and my fear that "this will be the moment that the gods of motivation forsake me." I also pay homage to my audience by declaring that "I'm overawed to be in the presence of such smart, accomplished people, but I'll get over it."

5. Build Rapport by Demonstrating Your Love of Others

Rapport means harmonious connection. It's when you experience a mutual empathy and understanding that makes communication clear and easy. It transcends surface differences to revel in the similarities within. There is no sense of belonging without it. It's a choice to search for the magic that each person brings to the relationship and celebrate it with them.

Rapport is activated and accelerated by the language of YBH. It brings common purpose and values to the surface. By expressing your love of others, it makes them love you back because the people you love most are the people who love you. Here are some of the phrases that are guaranteed to build rapport, especially when delivered with a smile (add your own):

- You really struck a chord with me when you...
- Now you're talking my language.
- You're clearly one of us now.
- We're totally aligned.
- I love how you seem to really get me.
- You nailed it. You said it exactly the way I wanted to.
- I'm grateful I get to work with you.
- Wow! You said what was in my head. How did you know that?
- When you said/did..., I knew we made the right choice to hire you.

6. Declare Your Absolute Support for Others—and Follow Through

The language of YBH all comes down to this: Can I trust your word? Will you protect me if I take a risk, give my all, and I still fail?

We can only face the future because of the people behind us. Our sense of belonging is directly proportionate to the security we derive from the collective. Loyalty is earned one commitment or one follow-through at a time. A single letdown can make others feel unsafe if it isn't satisfactorily communicated.

Every day is election day if you're campaigning for the support of the best people. Irrespective of your role or status, if you build a reputation as someone who is totally invested in the well-being and success of others, they will vote for you. It sounds obvious, but it's far from easy. Here are some of the phrases that will get you into the right offices:

- I've got your back.
- You've got my full support.
- I trust you.
- You can trust me to go above and beyond for you.
- My word is my bond.
- Your success is my success.
- Let's do this!

7. Work to Avoid Microaggressions

The South African Nobel Peace Prize laureate Desmond Tutu said, "Language does not describe reality. Language creates the reality that it describes." Well-chosen phrases cultivate camaraderie and boost belonging. Ill-chosen phrases betray bias, ignorance, or lack of cultural awareness. They may not just offend but add to existing hurts. And they can show the person who commits them in a bad light, too—like Diane's colleagues who assumed she was a server.

The *Merriam-Webster Dictionary* defines a microaggression as "a comment or action that subtly and often unconsciously or unintentionally expresses a prejudiced attitude toward a member of a marginalized group (such as a racial minority)." Despite a lack of intention or awareness, microaggressions can inflict pain and discomfort, even more so if the speaker demonstrates a lack of caring about the impact of their statement on the well-being or dignity of others.

One of the most blatant forms of this behaviour is when a man interrupts a woman mid-thought, before she's able to articulate her point, with the condescending phrase, "Well, actually, I think..." Men are nearly three times as likely to interrupt a woman than another man. The *New York Times* called men interrupting women "a universal phenomenon." And the kicker is when a man parrots the same idea as the woman he interrupted and gets all the credit for it. Elizabeth Ames, former senior vice president of programs, marketing, and alliances for the AnitaB.org, says this is one of the biggest workplace microaggressions she hears about.

Another common one is a statement like, "You look so young" or "You're too pretty to be an engineer." The comment focuses attention on someone's appearance rather than on their credentials, and it may subtly undermine their authority on the job. Remarking on someone's apparent youth or looks may also imply that they seem inexperienced or somehow unqualified for their job. What may be meant as a compliment can come across as a passive-aggressive insult.

The same applies when a white colleague tells a colleague of colour, "You're so articulate" or "You speak so well." The remark suggests that they assumed the person in question would be less articulate—and are surprised to find out they aren't.

On the other hand, a question like, "Do you even know what TikTok is?" expressed by a younger person to an older person implies that only those thirty-something or younger could possibly know about the latest social and technological trends. While joking about your grey-haired colleague's social media knowledge or acumen might not be ill-intended, in a workplace setting it can suggest a barrier between those who are "with it" and those who are "past it."

A classic faux pas is the question "Where are you *actually* from?" On the surface, asking someone about their ethnic heritage appears to be just a way to get to know someone. But for Latinos, Asians, and "people who fall in between the black-white racial binary in the United States," the question gets tiresome, as journalist Tanzina Vega wrote for CNN. "The next time you want to inquire about someone's race, ethnicity or national origin, ask yourself: Why do I want to know?" Vega wrote. "Or better yet, rather than asking anyone 'where are you really from?' try listening—or letting that person ask you a question—instead." Receiving that question again and again can imply that a person doesn't truly belong in their country, just because of their appearance.

It's easy to excuse ourselves for causing offence by uttering an ill-considered comment or using what we feel is a common phrase: "You're being too sensitive." In fact, what they are is sensitized, likely from past experience. And they clearly feel your comment is injurious. If you truly wish to create an environment where people feel safe, it's essential to consider that your life experience might be very different from others you work with. Listen thoughtfully and try to look at things from their perspective and experience. It will enrich you both, as well as your team and organization.

Seek to be an ally. If you say something that is experienced by a listener as offensive, apologize, regardless of your intention, acknowledge their concern, and view it as an opportunity to learn. The right words will come to you, but when I've said something that's caused offence, and we'll all do it at some point, I typically own it by contritely saying, "I'm sorry I offended you by my choice of words. It was never my intention to offend you. I'd be grateful if you would share what my words meant to you so I don't offend anyone else in the future."

And pass the favour on: quietly let others know of their discordant words so they can take appropriate action. If you're at the receiving end of the situation, try to assume good intent and alert the other person to their misspeak. As an agent of belonging, you need a trusted cadre of advisors who can coach you on the appropriate language and immediately correct you on your errant phrases. At a time when we're more polarized than most of us can remember, on more topics and in more areas, consider how lifting others up, rather than choosing to put them down, will undoubtedly create a more positive, safe, and productive environment.

2

Be the Keeper of the Safety Flame

THE PANDEMIC ushered in a new world disorder that can make even the most entrenched insiders feel like outsiders. As our external environment changes, our internal doubts multiply. My coaching clients often tell me, "This is not what I signed up for." Or "This place isn't what it used to be." Or "I'm not having as much fun as I used to have." What's more, high performers can be naturally paranoid. They are constantly alert to signals that they're slipping or losing their relevance—even when those signals only originate from inside their own heads. The curse of competence means never being completely comfortable.

Making others feel safe, however, can never be a function of whether or not *you* feel safe. Others' well-being cannot depend on your mood, outlook, or whims. It's your personal consistency that matters most to them. People often tell me that their biggest source of professional stress is the variability or unpredictability of their immediate boss. They spend so much of their energy determining the best time to approach them or the best way to navigate their boss's volatility that they have very little energy left to actually innovate or explore new ways of winning.

Being the Keeper of the Safety Flame means forgoing all excuses for not playing at your best. It calls for total ownership of the moment, irrespective of your position. For example, if you're the leader, you intentionally radiate a warmth and openness that draws people in. You express a relish for the role even though you may be battling with fatigue or frustration. If you're lower on the org chart, you ask questions or make comments that demonstrate your total engagement. You're not dissuaded by others' ennui or lukewarm commitments. You energize by example.

Develop Your Multiple Personality Agility

In 1599, Shakespeare wrote in his play *As You Like It*,

> All the world's a stage,
>
> And all the men and women merely players.
>
> They have their exits and their entrances,
>
> And one man in his time plays many parts

In that regard, nothing has changed in over 425 years. We're all players in the production called Our Life. So we need to perform like our lives depend on it. On the dark days, you need to bring the light. When the force isn't with you, you must act like it is.

I'm not telling you to "fake it until you make it." Faking anything will never radiate strength and confidence. I'm telling you to remind yourself of who you are when you're at your best and how much your team needs you to perform at that level. Then you need to consciously act like that. It takes courage, but courage is easier to muster when you have no alternative. If you hold yourself to the Keeper of the Safety Flame standard, you'll find ways to sustain it. You'll also discover that emotion comes from motion. Feel the way you act; don't act the way you feel. You have a role you have taken on—not on a stage but in real life. Live up to it when you are in it.

When Diane is playing the role of psychiatrist, she can listen to a patient's traumatic story and respond empathically, but with professional detachment. But when she's in personal mode, those same stories can reduce her to tears—she permits herself to give in to her emotions. We need to play our professional roles with all the composure that takes. As a psychiatrist, Diane processes inputs through different filters. She is both more sensitive to the data and insulated against it at the same time. She calls it *multiple personality agility*—the ability to move seamlessly between the various characters she needs to inhabit: doctor, friend, mother, student, author, wife, ambassador, commercial leader, changemaker. She enables the most appropriate character, or a compilation of the right ones, to come to the fore in each situation.

I am less skilled than Diane in this area. I'm often reminded by my wife that she is not my client and I need to communicate with her accordingly. Or I kick into selling mode with my friends when I want them to adopt my point of view. Or I may not express the requisite level of empathy with family members because I default to coaching rather than simply listening. That's one of the reasons I've loved writing this book with Diane—I'm learning on the fly. But

I know that, ultimately, what has an effect on others is not what I think but what I do.

We Are Judged Not by Our Feelings but by Our Actions

When Diane and I are in front of client audiences at marquee corporate or association events, we are held to three simple standards:

1. Did we inspire or empower people to do something that they otherwise would never have done?
2. Do they feel uplifted because they spent time in our company?
3. Would they recommend us to other colleagues or friends?

Unless we get an unqualified yes, yes, and yes, we have failed them. Our internal states of mind are invisible to others and irrelevant to their experience with us.

We are judged not by our feelings but by our actions. Others observe and evaluate our behaviours moment by moment. If we create a safe experience, they will risk doing or saying more. If we don't, they won't. The willingness of others to interact with us is the real test of our ability to create a space where they feel like they belong. Diane calls it a *compassionate culture*—an environment where people can share their ideas, excitement, and successes, but also their anxieties, upsets, and frustrations, without fear of retribution or humiliation.

Compassion goes a degree deeper than empathy. Empathy means sharing and understanding someone's pain or discomfort. Compassion means being committed to alleviating someone's pain or discomfort. It's the ability to take impactful action that makes all the difference. When compassion is your core motivation, you focus on others' well-being. You see things through their eyes, and you help make it right for them.

Sometimes compassion means coaching someone through a crisis or providing them with the support and resources to navigate through their struggle. Other times, compassion means not coaching or suggesting, but simply providing them the space to find their own answers so they truly own the win. Compassion can also mean helping someone exit the organization on their terms so you give them a soft landing. By supporting their narrative, they're less likely to light fires on the way out. You close out the relationship with civility and respect.

Diane has discovered that a compassionate culture builds her team's stamina and resilience. They know they will be supported. They know they will be treated fairly. They know Diane has their back. As a result they're willing to fail fast—which is critical for a technology start-up—work with agility, and experiment with creative solutions. They recover from mistakes faster and share lessons openly. They accelerate their path forward.

Obviously, there are moments when any of us will fall short of the Keeper of the Safety Flame standard. That always sucks. We reflect with frustration and castigate ourselves for being underwhelming. We feel guilty about not delivering a high return on trust. Sometimes, it's hard to let it go. But, as quickly as possible, we must shift gears and focus on what we've just learned. However hard it is to get over it, we can't let it keep us from playing at our best the next time. As Billy Jean King, the great tennis champion, said, "Champions keep playing until they get it right." I know it's not as easy as that makes it sound—I have a strong tendency to ruminate over mistakes that I believe I shouldn't have made. But the only way out of it is through it, so I focus on learning from it. As is often said, "This too shall pass."

THE QUICK WIN

Diane's been providing continuing medical education to her colleagues for more than twenty years. In fact, she describes teaching as her passion. Her colleagues are extremely busy, often burned out (so they're easily frustrated), and their time is precious, so she does everything possible to ensure they have an incredible experience at her events. She states, "Everyone has their own style when speaking to a group, which develops with time and experience. But reading the words on a slide verbatim, presenting in a dry, humourless fashion, or speaking in a derogatory or condescending manner turns everyone off, fast. Smile, be yourself (and laugh at yourself), and most importantly, deliver your content as a story. Have the audience walk through the story with you, sharing the emotions, anticipating the next steps, and listening for the pearls."

The next time you're preparing to face an audience, ask yourself these three questions, especially during difficult moments, and think about what it would take to earn the answer of yes, yes, and yes: Am I inspiring or empowering people to do something that they otherwise would never have done? Am I creating a space where others feel like they belong, irrespective of how I feel? Do they feel safer because they work with me?

3

Create Belonging in a Hybrid Reality

BELONGING DOESN'T DEPEND on being in the same space. But it can be affected by it, as so many of us discovered when our working environment changed abruptly in 2020. Literally going somewhere where you are needed is a signal that you belong there. Your office or worksite was your second place after your home. Whether it was hard labour or a labour of love, it was an activity you performed with other people who were engaged in a similar mission, under similar conditions. The water cooler or the coffee station were opportunities to gossip, commiserate, or celebrate, depending on the day. Even the sounds and smells were familiar cues that indicated normality.

Technology has untethered us from the physical office, but it has also increased our sense of isolation and separateness from each other. Physical proximity creates serendipitous encounters. However, if we're working remotely, unless meetings are scheduled, they don't occur. And even when they do, there is a lack of spontaneity or fun that can make them productive. It's hard to know when to speak or jump in when we can't sense the cues that prompt us one way or the other. Our social skills are rusting while our inertia is increasing. Home is sticky. Getting out is tricky. It can feel much easier to just stay put.

But get out we must. Creating belonging means constantly checking in with your constituents, both online and in person. It means being accountable for others' well-being. It means you are always the initiator. You don't give up if you don't get a response. Silence just means you have to find another way to get through. If someone is a part of your ecosystem, they must never feel like they don't matter or like you don't care. It can be exhausting, but it can also be exhilarating, especially when others tell you how much your contribution meant to them. As Diane says, leadership is not a title—it's a responsibility to each other.

A virtual meeting may be the least intuitive thing we can do: talk to a patchwork of miniature faces and blank squares on a screen, while we watch ourselves talking to them, and manipulate a PowerPoint deck, and track the chat responses, and type our replies, and engage in live conversations with people who are multi-tasking or otherwise barely engaged, while our dogs bark or beg to be let out and our kids wander in and out of the room, demanding to be fed. Even worse is the silence that follows our presentation when there are no hands raised or comments made. We're often left feeling like we're on the precipice of nothingness, speaking into the void.

Attending a virtual meeting can feel just as alienating. Hour after hour, day after day, we try to listen and engage with others as they soldier valiantly on. Sometimes they're clear and audible. Other times, they look like they're in a witness protection program, muffled voice and off camera, so we're left staring at an odd emoji or a picture of their cat.

Hybrid meetings are worse—half of the team is online and unable to interact, because the other half is there in person, able to engage more seamlessly, read the room, and not have to search for the "hand up" icon when they want to speak. Most of us have spoken for five to ten seconds before realizing we've been on mute and no one noticed we were speaking. Diane recalls a talk she gave mid-pandemic, where she spoke for more than five minutes before someone finally managed to find her cell number and tell her she had disconnected from the meeting.

We've been told to keep our cameras on, but we prefer to switch them off so we can multi-task undetected. We try the best we can to engage and even contribute to meetings, but after a few hours of them, it's all but impossible. And yet, for many of us, it's still better than commuting to the office where there's no place to mute or hide. At least we're in the safety and comfort of home while we navigate the twilight zone. Work from home solves more problems than it creates, although we do miss the camaraderie of our colleagues sometimes. And that's when we go into the office or visit our clients—two or three days a week.

Virtual rejection is easy to do, but hard to take. "Meeting declined" is like a mild rejection—especially if it's someone with whom you really want to speak. Getting ghosted is also an irritation, along with last-minute cancellations and reschedules. And, of course, there are always internet failures that happen just as you're about to go for the close or make your killer comments.

The key is to make meetings with you meaningful. No matter what the topic, others must reap a high return on their investment—an ROI—of taking the time to meet with you. They must be moved, touched, or inspired in some way. When your name comes up on their screen, it must spell possibility, success, reward, luck, growth, or opportunity. There must be a spike of dopamine when they see you because interacting with you is a pleasure or a relief in a world too often filled with frustration or tension.

THE QUICK WIN

Diane's team isn't just spread across the country, they're all over the world. Like all tech start-ups, decisions and changes happen at lightning speed, which requires disciplined, effective communication. As she states, "Meetings are one of the greatest challenges I've faced as a leader. As our product develops, our needs change, so we can't agree on a process or type of meeting and stick to it forever—we need to constantly reflect on whether we have the right meeting structure, attendees, timing, and use of resources. In the past, we've waited too long to pivot and create a new meeting plan because everything seemed just fine, until it suddenly occurred to us that it wasn't!" But there is a consistent meeting hygiene Diane has developed to make the virtual world less painful—starting and ending on time, ensuring there's one "meeting owner" who's responsible for the hygiene, starting at five minutes after the hour to allow for bio breaks—all things that respect her teammates, who are glued to their screens all day. And when her entire team comes together for their monthly virtual meeting, they've set aside the first ten minutes for kudos—personal expressions of gratitude between teammates. It's an opportunity to thank someone (or a group) publicly for going above and beyond, and her team's feedback is clear—it nurtures belonging.

Commit to at least three in-person or remote meetings a week, even if it's just a quick check-in, with the single objective of enhancing others' sense of belonging. Intentionally make every meeting with you, in person or online, a pleasurable experience—whatever it takes. Catch yourself when you're just going through the motions. Ask for feedback about how you can make them better.

1. Repeat Your Raison d'Être Relentlessly
2. Commit to Optimizing Communication
3. Be an Authentic Actor
4. Master the Technology
5. Tell a Great Story
6. Animate Your Style
7. Listen Like You Are All In
8. Recover Quickly

8 PROVEN GUIDELINES FOR CREATING BELONGING IN A HYBRID REALITY

OVER THE LAST three years, Diane and I have experimented exhaustively with a range of different techniques and approaches to create belonging in a hybrid reality. We've studied what really works and what doesn't. The result is the following eight proven guidelines that you can begin applying immediately. Try them out. Make them your own by adding your secret sauce.

1. Repeat Your Raison d'Être Relentlessly

Seize every opportunity to declare the most important reason or purpose for your existence as a person or enterprise. *Remind* is a powerful verb. It means bringing information back into focus for the listener—for a moment, the reminder makes the content top of mind.

The conscious pursuit of your purpose can make the difference between winning or losing. Being purposeful means having or showing determination or resolve, while purposeless means having no aim or plan. It's binary. Purposeful will beat purposeless every day of the week. If you and your team don't have a purpose or forget your purpose—your reason for being—your success will be limited.

Your purpose should not articulate what you make or do—it should say what you stand for. Just focusing on a product or service is a trap: with the speed of change, especially on the technology front, establishing what you stand for—why you exist—enhances your ability to adapt and grow. Instead of being limited by what you do, your purpose should reflect *what you could do*. Establishing a purpose can also inform what you don't or shouldn't do.

The stronger your raison d'être, the stronger your future. If you and your team have a meaningful reason for getting up every morning, you'll make progress every day. You won't be deterred by the inevitable missteps and setbacks that are the currency of life. What's more, you'll support the development of their own raison d'être.

According to Gallup, only 13 percent of US employees believe their leaders communicate effectively. And just 15 percent strongly agree that their organization's leadership makes them feel enthusiastic about the future. That's why people don't feel a sense of safety in the present. It's impossible to feel secure in an environment that isn't enthusiastic about its future. That's why Diane focuses on her enterprise's mission in every meeting:

> With misdiagnosis rates between 66 percent and 98 percent for psychiatric patients treated in primary care, the lack of a consistent, evidence-based "standard of care" is shockingly evident. Our mission is to dramatically improve mental health outcomes, so my team's core purpose is to "create a world where optimal health

care decisions are made with confidence and compassion." Once our purpose was established, we went on to consider how to deliver on that purpose, by setting goals, big and small, all rooted in our core purpose.

Every time I speak to Diane, she expresses her passion for her purpose in a way that makes me want to be even more involved with her work. Her company's purpose is a true and meaningful expression of what they want to do, so she and her entire team believe in it. Throughout this book, we openly commit to our joint purpose with you: to grow leaders that make people feel like they belong so they realize their full potential, become their best self, and pay it forward, helping others to do the same.

What's your professional purpose? If you don't have one, it's time to create one. Remember: Your purpose needs to inspire both you and your team. It must be big, broad, and enduring (will it still stand in ten, twenty, or fifty years?), and it needs to answer the question "What could we do?" not "What do we do?" How can you share it with others so that they become enthusiastic about their future?

2. Commit to Optimizing Communication

Communicate your commitment to staying in touch. Set up a cadence of meetings that is sacrosanct. Hold people accountable to attend and actively participate. Hold yourself accountable for making them want to attend. Bring so much to each meeting that others don't dare miss them. If people don't attend, follow up with a reminder that they were missed and that their participation is crucial to the success of the group.

At the same time, set up "catch-up meetings" with team members, aimed entirely at enabling them to share issues that are personal to them, whether it's a crisis or a potential opportunity. They could simply be a check-in, but in those situations, a broader "Tell me about how your work is going" will yield more fruitful feedback than "How's it going?" which might result in a vague response. The point is to give others the chance to verbalize what's important to them and demonstrate your willingness to support them as they manage a challenge.

If you don't maintain the social connection, you'll miss an opportunity to understand how they are being influenced by their environment, at work and at home. A real sense of connection can nurture their commitment, creativity, and feeling of value as a team member. They become more invested in their teammates, the organization's purpose, and in you. When others open up to you, they are expressing their trust in you. Be a vault; a failure to maintain confidentiality may never be overcome.

It's always your responsibility to keep the connection alive. Without your active endeavours, entropy will take hold. Connections will wither. People will lose touch with each other. Cohesion will crumble. On the other hand, remember that people value rituals and patterns of predictability in their lives. As the orchestrator and owner of meaningful meetings, you can give that to them.

3. Be an Authentic Actor

You have a role to play, so play it like an Academy Award–winning actor would play it. Be you, but be the best you that you can be, even when you're not feeling your best. You don't have to be on all the time but you do have to be on when it counts. Remember that you are a brand—you represent a promise that you are making to others. You're only as valuable as your ability to fulfill that promise. There will be moments when you don't feel like bringing the heat. Those are the moments that will make or break you. Other people don't care about what you feel like doing that day. They care about how you make them feel that day.

Paradoxically, being an authentic actor can liberate you from your own social anxiety. For example, if you're an introvert but you need to act like an extrovert on occasion, knowing that you're acting helps you deal with your introversion. If I'm nervous when I'm about to give a keynote talk, I act as though I'm confident. My feelings follow my actions.

Diane is in constant listener mode. When she wears her psychiatrist hat, she needs to get into a state of total immersion in her patients' needs. She intentionally visualizes a box into which she places all her distractions, knowing that she will get back to them after the appointment. On the other hand, when she is with her RAPIDS team, her roles include focuser-in-chief and guardian-of-the-culture. She is continually reminding her team about their purpose, the values they've agreed on, and the importance she places on a compassionate culture. She says, "I try to keep things light, and take myself lightly, but I am uncompromising on purpose, values, and culture. If I don't embody foundational elements every day, I've broken a solemn promise."

No matter how skilled an authentic actor you become, there will always be people who don't like your style. It might be a bitter pill to swallow, but you can't be everyone's cup of tea. As a presenter, if I'm doing my job, most people will be actively engaged. I don't focus on the one or two people who seem disengaged and would prefer to be anywhere else. I remind myself that I don't have insight into their apparent disengagement—they might have had a fender-bender on their way to the event—and I focus on my fans and advocates. You'll have a greater fan base if you sustain your passion for the topic. No one will ever doubt Diane's knowledge, conviction, and commitment to the effective treatment of mental illness—and the removal of the stigma that it carries. She speaks with passion and confidence. If she was vague or wishy-washy, no one would listen.

And here's one more decisive insight: if you are an outsider, you can be as influential as an insider, maybe even more so. You have the perspective to see things hidden from their view. You have license to say things that insiders cannot. I know from experience. As a South African Canadian who is contracted to deliver a keynote or perform a coaching assignment, I'm always the outsider. But my statements carry disproportionate weight because of it. What's more, I've discovered that even insiders can feel like outsiders when they're challenging the status quo.

4. Master the Technology

As the Keeper of the Safety Flame, you must make it easy for people to see and listen to you. Your webcam should be 4k. Your sound should be crystal clear. Your internet connection should be strong and consistent. Your virtual presentation skills should be sound. Even when you're engaging people from a hotel room, you need to be crisp and sharp. That means travelling with a 4k webcam and even a portable light. Remember, your last meeting is the most important one. If people dial into a meeting with you, they must have a satisfying experience. If you need guidance, it's available in abundant supply.

Don't make people struggle to communicate with you. In a day filled with unsatisfactory meetings, you don't want to make your meeting another unnecessary challenge—especially when it is so easy to make it a great experience.

5. Tell a Great Story

Grab your participants' attention from the get-go. Let them know why they will benefit from the call. Make it interesting. Earn the right to be heard no matter what your title or familiarity with the audience. Use people's natural curiosity in your favour. We're all beginners and students in this new time.

Tell people what you plan to share and then tell your story. Make it tight and compelling. Few people have the ability to seam together a story without thinking about it ahead of time, but with practice, you'll learn how to stay focused but also to have the flexibility to inject your own lightness and experience into your narrative. There is power in gentle repetition, being able to come back to a great point (especially if it got a laugh), and ending on a high note, especially if it's a call to action. You want people to leave your meeting or presentation inspired, with a clear sense of why and next steps. "That's an hour I'll never get back" is a dagger you'll never face if you plan to engage. Yes, there is a lot of preparation required, but it's worth it. Every presentation matters.

Think about the presentations and meetings that you enjoy the most: it's when there is a clear narrative that is well told and skillfully explored. The structure should suit the time available for the meeting. A quick sprint should be calibrated differently from a lengthier walk through the material. No matter what the content, your job is to make it interesting. There is an inherent drama in every message—your job is to find it.

In his book *Winning on Purpose: The Unbeatable Strategy of Loving Customers*, Fred Reichheld begins with this riveting sentence: "Just a few weeks before my sixty-fifth birthday, I awoke from an anesthesia induced sleep to hear

You are always 100% responsible for making the meeting a rewarding experience.

my doctor pronounce six dreaded words: You have a large malignant tumor." Reichheld goes on to share why he was willing to dedicate whatever time he had left to completing the book. With that kind of start, you can't help but want to discover why he was so motivated to write it. And by the way, he didn't disappoint.

Here is a simple five-point template that will enable you to get your points across with clarity and brevity:

1. **The Challenge:** What specific problem or crisis needed to be resolved?
2. **The Response:** What actions were taken?
3. **The Outcome:** What results were achieved?
4. **The Lesson:** What lessons were learned?
5. **The Call to Action:** What things should you do differently?

6. Animate Your Style

Whether you're an introvert, ambivert, or extrovert, energize your delivery by using your face, voice, and body to enliven your presentation. If that's not your usual style, try to imagine yourself as someone else and imbue them with these attributes. Smile. Speak at least 20 percent louder than you would normally talk. Speaking more loudly tends to slow your pace and can radiate greater confidence. Finish your sentences with an exclamation point.

Use your hands to punctuate your delivery. A webcam can act as a natural suppressor. That means it's reducing your natural warmth and spontaneity. So, ham it up a little. It may seem awkward at first, but you will very quickly get into a new rhythm. Pretend that you are the host of a reality TV show. Have some fun. This is *Survivor* or *The Amazing Race* for real. And speaking of reality shows, just like any good host, look directly at the camera as often as you can, rather than looking at the people on your screen. This makes it seem, for each audience member, that you're looking directly at them, which is more engaging. Yes, you may not see their non-verbal reaction to your words as you say them, but you stand a much greater chance of moving them in your desired direction. You can look at them when they react to your comments.

The same principles of animation, warmth, and spontaneity apply whether you're presenting online or in person. All our research shows that the more authentic and empathetic you appear to be, the more likely others will be to listen to you. It's never just about the facts. It's about how you make them feel.

Ask a coach to provide you with candid feedback. It's impossible to see yourself objectively. You need the informed perspective of an educated outsider. One of my clients told me that the insights I provided her completely changed her approach to presenting. She's discovered her inner thespian. She now looks forward to hosting calls and presenting from the stage. Her followership has also increased dramatically.

7. Listen Like You Are All In

Nothing signals safety like total engagement. When others feel heard, they feel validated. When they feel that you're interested in what they say, they feel like *they're* interesting to you. They are immediately saved from their two biggest fears: being boring or sounding stupid.

When others are speaking, show your rapt attention. Demonstrate your empathy. Ask relevant questions. Make appropriate comments. If the speaker asks for feedback, give it to them. Make sure they feel validated by your participation. Don't leave them hanging. Be the one that goes first—the speaker will never forget your generosity. Resist the temptation to look at your cell phone or multi-task. If you're online, keep your camera on and be aware of your facial expressions—maintain a look that says you really want to be there. Diane and her partner at RAPIDS have worked together on various projects for more than a decade. He admitted to her that he's very sensitive to her facial expressions—if she seems frustrated or unhappy, he gets really distracted. Diane wasn't even aware he was reacting to her expressions, and mostly he was reading them wrong. She says, "When I concentrate, I can look stern, which for him was jarring during virtual meetings, because I'm usually smiling. We decided, to help him to maintain focus, to have a 'safe word'—if he thinks I look grumpy, he says, 'Diane, peach.' It immediately makes me smile and soften my expression. It also made me aware of how my expressions can impact how others feel, especially virtually, when they see only my face."

Whatever your past experience with others, listen to them freshly in every conversation. Don't bring yesterday's judgements or disappointments to today's interaction. Even when you're forced to talk to people you don't particularly like, look for the breakthrough that could occur if you struck the right chord in this conversation.

I'm not suggesting you should be naive. I'm inviting you to get the most out of the time you spend with the full gamut of people in your life. If you don't change your approach, you condemn yourself to groundhog days of frustration and futility. And once again remember: You are always 100 percent responsible for making the meeting a rewarding experience—what would that take?

The most important part of a substantive conversation is not the topic—it's your response, psychologists say. Show the other person that you understand and care for them.

You can do this by saying some version of "I'm so glad you shared this with me." If you don't understand, respectfully seek clarification. If you listen with the intent to understand, not solely to respond, you enable the other person to articulate their own breakthroughs.

8. Recover Quickly

No matter how prepared you are, you're going to stumble, hesitate, or go astray at some point—whether you're online or in person. That's OK, but don't get stuck. Just carry on. It only makes you human. Your audience may not even notice. And even if they do, they'll forgive you, especially if you recover quickly. Composure does gain you kudos, but if you're too polished, you may be branded as slick or superficial.

On March 4, 2023, Chris Rock performed his new Netflix stand-up special, *Selective Outrage*. The *New York Times* said that it had "moments that felt emotional, messy, and fierce. It was the least rehearsed, most riveting material in an uneven hour. Rock is a perfectionist who has always exhibited a meticulous sense of control. But in *Selective Outrage*, he even botched a key part of one joke, getting the title of a movie wrong. Normally, such an error would have been edited out, but since this was the first live global event in the history of Netflix, Rock could only stop, call attention to it and tell the joke again. It messed up his momentum, but the trade-off might have been worth it since the flub added an electric spontaneity and unpredictability that was a drawing card."

What works for Chris Rock will work for you. The most polished pre-recorded message is no match for an imperfect live one. Prepare all you can, then just do the best you can. Jerry Seinfeld, another seasoned comedian, jokes about how much people hate public speaking, pointing out that at a funeral, most people would rather be in the coffin than give the eulogy. That means your audience will empathize with you and root for your success.

THE QUICK WIN

Like almost everyone, Diane and I lived our professional lives entirely online through the pandemic. Now, with new hybrid workstyles, those experiences have proved invaluable for sustaining valued relationships, building business opportunities, and developing our networks far beyond what we could have imagined. As Diane now believes, "Effective virtual communication is a vital professional skill." And, as you'll quickly discover, it's also critical when your job is to create belonging in a hybrid reality.

Over the next eight days, intentionally use each of the eight proven guidelines for creating belonging in a hybrid reality to alchemize instant rapport. Gauge what works best for you. Then go deeper and get better at it. Explore what it takes to become a master at creating belonging in a hybrid reality.

I

Creating Belonging in a Hybrid World

III

Owning Your Power

II

Growing Enriching Relationships

Winning on the Brink

V

Showing the Way

PART II

GROWING ENRICHING RELATIONSHIPS

4

Change Your Rules for Relatedness

EVERY RELATIONSHIP requires making a deposit on someone's sense of belonging. To relate to someone means establishing a connection to them by showing your sincere interest in them. If you're alone in a new city and you meet someone with whom you form a friendship, you immediately feel less like a stranger and more like a member of a community. No one actually wants to be a stranger. It's simply a state we must pass through to become someone who belongs to the place in which they're situated. Even tourists don't want to be called tourists. They want to be temporary residents of their chosen destinations.

The need for belonging creates and sustains relationships. No matter what the relationship, it requires constant attention to help it grow. Familiarity will only breed contentment when shared values, attitudes, and actions are consistently repeated. If you want to enjoy the fruits, you must water the roots.

When you learn anything, your brain creates new connections between brain cells, which is like new electrical wiring, that eventually makes the new information or activity part of your repertoire. The reason "practice makes perfect" is because repeating a new behaviour strengthens those connections, making it easier to do. Unfortunately, the new wiring isn't reserved just for learning something that's good or helpful, like a new language or riding a bike. If you've learned dysfunctional coping skills, the wiring that results from repetition can make those habits more entrenched and harder to stop, even though they're unhealthy and ineffective. For example, if you tend to avoid important but difficult conversations because you're uncomfortable with conflict, your brain has been wired to use avoidance because it provides short-term comfort or security, despite the risk of causing significant medium- or long-term problems.

According to Diane, how we interact with others, build relationships, and manage our emotional responses, especially to conflict, is determined by many factors. "One factor is temperament—babies are born with their own, innate way of reacting to the world. Temperament isn't learned, it's completely genetic. Some of us were easygoing babies (predictable, approachable, adaptable), others were really cranky (unpredictable, uncomfortable in novel situations, fearful of new people), and the rest of us were somewhere in between. And even the most loving parents, working together and providing the best possible home life, can't make a clingy, avoidant, unpredictable baby into an easy one. I've tried! But they can create an environment that helps their temperamental baby to prosper. That's because our environment—how we're parented, our education, our friendships, and our exposure to other enriching experiences—has a massive impact on how we think, feel, and behave."

Regardless of your life circumstances, you might still struggle with creating or maintaining healthy relationships, whether personal or professional. But if you're aware of this challenge, which means you have the insight to recognize this is a barrier for you, there are many paths to improving your relationship IQ, which will undoubtably foster your future success.

It's not fair but it's true—the way you were parented shapes the way you manage your relationships, at work and at home. Your parents were your role models. Diane has treated countless patients who had a highly narcissistic parent, causing them to spend their entire lives trying to make their parent love them. In the workplace, they may have projected unmet needs onto colleagues and desperately tried to please them. I am also that sort of person. I have an inordinate desire to please that emanated from the impossibility of pleasing my mother, or my father, who passed when I was sixteen years old.

The skills we learn as children are what make us the adults we become. If you're lucky, you learned about respect, empathy, compassion, caring, acceptance, love, adaptability, responsibility, and discipline. If not, these values may have been missing in action—Diane calls it being "unparented." Or even worse, you may have been afflicted by their opposites, as is sadly the case for children raised by a domineering, narcissistic, or antisocial parent. Both Diane and I grew up in chaos. I replicated some of the chaos in my own family before my wife, Hilary, helped me to reshape my behaviours. I was an impaired Peter Pan, addicted to the adrenalin of acclaim and success. It was her strength, resilience, and love that enabled our family to survive and thrive. To this day, she is the matriarchal figure around which the extended family revolves. I am the source of income and interesting stories. It's taken a lifetime to get here, but now it works beautifully.

Diane responded to her chaotic upbringing very differently. As a parent, she felt driven not to replicate her own childhood. She over-demonstrated her love for her children to the point where they had to ask her to stop worrying so much about their happiness. She was so overinvested in having a harmonious relationship with her children that it made it difficult for them to express normal frustrations. It took a direct, heartfelt appeal from her daughter to free Diane from the fear of losing her love. Like me, Diane was fortunate to have an incredible parenting partner. Her husband had the opposite childhood experience, providing a rudder for their family that kept them afloat and on course, even in the roughest seas.

Many adults are relationship impaired because of how they were parented and other important childhood experiences. Just being aware of these powerful formative forces is a big step to resolving their negative impact. It's possible to learn how to relate to others, personally and professionally, in a more effective, engaging, and constructive manner. Learning to understand and control your own thoughts, feelings, and behaviours, and recognizing that you cannot control anyone else, are foundational adult experiences. If you're struggling with building, nurturing, or maintaining personal or professional relationships, there are many resources available, depending on the challenge. Professional coaches can help with skill development, while a psychologist or clinical counsellor can help you to reframe negative childhood experiences and reduce their impact on your adult life.

When you look back at past behaviours that you might consider shameful or embarrassing, remember that most people don't remember or care. As Eleanor Roosevelt stated so eloquently, "You wouldn't worry so much about what others think of you if you realized how seldom they do." That's because they're thinking about themselves, their own lives, and their own past. It's time to stop torturing yourself over past indiscretions that others probably don't remember or see in the same way.

Build the Strength of Weak Ties

A key theme throughout this book is that you are a function of the people you surround yourself with—both in terms of your inner circle and your outer network. Your inner circle empowers you at your core. Your outer network creates opportunities by connecting you with people and information that wouldn't otherwise have been accessible. Mark Granovetter branded this concept "the strength of weak ties" and argued that, while strong ties (i.e., close relationships with friends and family) are important for emotional support, weak ties (i.e., more distant or casual relationships) are more valuable in terms of providing access to new information and opportunities.

According to the weak tie theory, an individual's strong ties are typically composed of people who are similar to them in terms of demographics, values, and interests. These individuals tend to share a lot of the same information and resources, and as a result, they are not likely to be sources of novel or diverse information. In contrast, weak ties are typically composed of people who are less like us and who have access to different social circles and networks, making them more likely to be sources of novel and diverse information. This can be especially valuable for individuals looking to find a new job or exploring new professional horizons.

It's always thrilling when a member of your outer network, a "weak tie," introduces you to an opportunity out of the blue. As a professional speaker and coach, I'm always foraging for new opportunities. About half of the time, I'm actively reaching out to both new prospects and members of my established network. But for the other half, my network reaches out to me with the gift of possibility. I never know when it's going to happen, but I count on it. That's why I spend almost a third of my time cultivating close connections, which maximizes the possibility of them bringing me new opportunities.

Here are five ways to grow your network—in person or online:

1. **Be recommended:** Leverage existing connections to make new ones. Prospects are much more likely to respond to you if a mutual acquaintance introduces you. Don't be afraid to ask existing members of your network to recommend you. They want to help you.
2. **Play up your similarities:** Showcase the values, interests, or priorities that you have in common. Make the prospect feel safe with you even before you connect.
3. **Bring value:** Come prepared with insights or information that the prospect is likely to find valuable. It should relate to your work or ways in which you can enrich their lives. You need to give value before you can expect to get value.
4. **Compliment them:** Find ways to genuinely flatter prospects that you can support with observations or data. We all appreciate credible kudos.
5. **Be persistent:** It may take multiple attempts to motivate prospects to respond. Don't give up. I often reach out ten or twenty times before I receive a response.

According to demographic research, 40 percent of Americans live by themselves, while 30 percent of Canadians live alone. There is clear data indicating that the greatest support for mental health, and protection against mental illnesses, is your constellation of social support networks. These are the people with whom you have affinity, and include both your inner circle and outer network. They are people who share your values and stand ready to help you navigate even in the roughest waters. Being around people who love and understand you is powerful medicine. That's why it's so important to get out there and meet your brain twins face to face. Virtual connections can only take you so far. Visceral connections need close physical proximity.

THE QUICK WIN

Using the five ways to grow your network, over the next week, ask five members of your current network to recommend you to someone in their group. At the same time, reach out to five prospects and reactivate your relationship with five people who have dropped off your contact list.

1. **Treat Yourself the Way You Want Others to Treat You**
2. **Bring People Joy**
3. **Give Much More Than You Receive**
4. **Fight Fair**
5. **Clarify and Contractualize Mutual Commitments**
6. **Own Everyone's Success but Accept Their Failures**

THE 6 RULES FOR RELATIONSHIP HEALTH

THERE ARE RULES to navigating and creating robust, reciprocal, rewarding relationships. As a psychiatrist, Diane is constantly exploring how to heal damaged relationships and the people who are hurt by them. As an executive coach, I'm endlessly studying how highly effective leaders at all levels master complex, matrixed relationships while they keep growing and caring for their own needs. Together, we've identified six rules for relationship health—in the home-space and the workplace.

1. Treat Yourself the Way You Want Others to Treat You

In 2021, Nashville Predators prospect Luke Prokop shared that he was gay in a social media post, making him the first player under contract to an NHL team to do so. His announcement was received positively by family, friends, and teammates. But that acceptance wasn't a given. In the year leading up to his announcement, Luke struggled under the immense pressure of his secret. In the end, he had a choice to make about his mental health and he decided he had to be his true self, no matter the cost. Luke now plays with a new freedom, knowing that he can be who he is—on and off the ice.

Together with Corey Hirsch, Diane interviewed Luke on her podcast *Blindsided*. "I don't want to have to walk into the gym or to the arena or just to practice, and keep thinking, 'Who knows? Who doesn't?' This is who I am." Prokop continued, "It's been very special, talking to my friends, my family, my coaches, my agents. And them being very supportive, me coming out and being OK with who I was. I've noticed myself being a lot more confident on the ice. Being able to truly be who I am. This is the best I've ever felt in the summer, and I think a large part of that is due to this process of me coming out. I'm not naive. I know there's going to be people who question it and get upset about my decision. But I have a really good group of people around me who can support me."

Like Prokop, we all need to honour our authentic self. If we don't champion ourselves, how can we expect others to? If you're ambivalent or negative about yourself, no other relationship is going to be at its best, because you aren't at your best. It can take a lifetime of pain and confusion to reach the point of self-belief. Diane and I have both been on that journey, and you probably have as well because it's a journey we're all taking. It has no finish line. Every day, we discover new things about ourselves. And every day, we need to remind ourselves why we're the friend we want to keep. We need to remember all the ways we've brought value to the people in our lives and forgive ourselves for when we didn't. Today is the best opportunity to be the person you've always wanted to be.

Diane is leading a growing team that is working to change the world by developing an innovative mental health technology, called RAPIDS. As a psychiatrist, she's the medical brains behind RAPIDS, but her vision and expertise are delivered through a technology built by coders, developers, and other innovation experts. "I can tell you *what* RAPIDS does," she shares, "but I can't explain exactly *how* it does it!" Her pride in her team is evident when she speaks about what they've been able to do, but even more so when she talks about the compassionate culture they're building. "I've learned that my team really didn't care what I knew until they knew that I truly cared," she says. "They are all experts in their own areas, and yes, I'm an expert in psychiatry, but that didn't really impact their lives. However, when I expressed my honest desire to help people access mental health care and ensure what we provided was the highest quality possible, that was important. They also needed to believe that I truly cared about them, as my teammates. This meant more than just saying the right words—I need to demonstrate, in every interaction, my commitment to our culture and each member of our team. This approach is entirely rooted in my desire to create a culture I want to work within—I treat my teammates like I'd want to be treated. What could be easier than that?"

2. Bring People Joy

Do other people enjoy their relationship with you? Do they want to be around you? If they could, would they spend more time with you? Are you an ongoing source of delight? Or are you a source of stress—someone to be endured rather than embraced? Are you aware of your impact on others, or do you indulge yourself at the expense of others?

The joy you bring can look different for each person and each situation, depending on the role you play in their lives. In each moment, the ultimate question is: Am I trying to lift others up or am I actually bringing them down? The vast majority of people don't wake up wanting to make others miserable. However, we can have that effect on others through our lack of insight, sensitivity, or empathy. All three deficits appear when we're preoccupied solely with our own well-being. If you are egocentric—thinking only of yourself without regard to the feelings or desires of others—you won't be a purveyor of joy. At best, you'll be tolerated. At worst, you'll be excluded.

Some people are naturally warm and sunny. Others may be inherently reserved or socially anxious. On the surface they may appear to be frosty, aloof, or unfriendly, but that is rarely the case. It's their natural introversion or the weight of anxiety that makes it challenging for them to seem comfortable or exude warmth, especially with new people and large groups. No matter where you are on the social skills spectrum, you can bring people joy by understanding what they want and addressing their needs. Some of my most rewarding relationships are with people who, on the surface, are the antithesis of my style. However, on the inside, they know what I want and they strive to meet my needs. In return, I know what they want and I return the favour. So, ask yourself: What do the most valuable people in my inner circle and outer network want, and how can I give them what they need?

At a foundational level, always appear happy to see someone and willing to help them. Express your enthusiasm in a way that matches your style. Listen attentively, so they feel heard. Demonstrate your empathy by feeding back to them their comments to you in their own words—"So what I hear you saying is..." or "Let me make sure I understand, your request is..." Respond to them in a manner that demonstrates their priorities are your priorities.

One of my most important clients is a woman I'll call Juliette. She is the CEO of a large manufacturing company. She is concerned about a senior executive on her team—

I'll call him Dave—who is struggling to adapt to change by resisting it. Juliette is a focused, buttoned-down, bottom-line kind of person. She cuts straight to the chase in every conversation. Here's how I responded to her in a recent conversation about Dave: "Juliette, thank you for reaching out to me. It means a lot. I am thrilled to work with Dave. I know how crucial he is to the success of your new program and I'm totally committed to helping him embrace the change. I know I can make a difference with him, just like I have with so many others." And by the way, Dave and I are making great progress.

On a personal level, your closest relationships—where you derive the most joy—can be with people who are very different from you. Diane and her husband are very different people. Diane is animated and not afraid of being silly. Her husband, Stuart, is more reflective and calmer. People feel heard by him and safe around him. Diane believes their differences have helped her to be a better person, because she's learned so much from watching him interact with others, personally and professionally. My wife, Hilary, is also very different from me. She is about making things. I'm about studying things. But what brings us together is far greater than what sets us apart. She is the yin to my yang.

3. Give Much More Than You Receive

When you pop out of the womb, you're totally dependent on someone else to clean you, feed you, comfort you, and keep you safe. And you give little back in return, except disruption and dirty diapers. In your early years, it's entirely understandable for that self-centeredness to continue, especially if you grew up in inhospitable circumstances. *Survival* means "the act or fact of living or continuing longer than another person or thing." Young people who grow up in chaos or neglect can come to view life as a zero-sum game where one person must lose in order for the other to win. When you're surrounded by scarcity, you take all you can before someone else takes it away.

As we mature, most of us, if we're lucky, discover the gift of helping others. We begin to appreciate the power and the pleasure of giving, and we start to understand the value of being valuable to others. We recognize the reciprocity that flows from contributing to the quality of another person's life. It's an incredible asset to have a reputation for generosity. One day, someone will take advantage of your generous nature. They may refuse to reciprocate, perhaps revealing themselves to be serial takers. Even worse, they may make false promises that put you in a precarious position. That's when you need to make a decision: to keep on being a giver or revert to being a taker. It's the choice between retaining your idealism or collapsing into cynicism. How often have you heard cynical people make statements like "No good deed goes unpunished," or "That'll teach me to help people"?

If you're willing to give, others will be tempted to take without any intention of giving back. You will be conned, cheated, and stolen from, and you'll regret your faith, your trust, or your naivete. You will maybe even curse, shout, or cry (or all three at once). But you will also be astonished by how much others want to give back to you. You will marvel at the miracles caused by great people making great things happen for you. You will be struck by how many more givers than takers you experience in your life. Ultimately, you'll realize that very little of worth happens without givers banding together in pursuit of common goals.

Diane shared a time when she was victimized by a smooth-talking psychopath who said all the right things:

When things are tightest, be your most generous.

I'll support you. I have your back. I believe in what you're doing. "I remember being so angry with myself, because I felt like a fool. I had not only risked my own professional standing, I had put others at risk, too. I'm a psychiatrist, for God's sake! I knew better and I should have listened to my gut, but I wanted to trust him. I gave myself the hardest time for the longest time, but then I realized I didn't want to become the kind of person who isn't able to trust, views everyone with suspicion, and loses the joy that comes from their professional journey. More than anything, I didn't want to give that creep another ounce of control in my life. So, I learned from the experience and then I let it go."

The most reassuring thing you can do for all the givers on your team is to demonstrate that you will never take their giving for granted. When things are tightest, be your most generous. In the companies with which I work, people remember how they were treated during COVID. It was a life-defining moment. They remember the compassion and support they received. Their engagement surged. Now they're giving back by going the extra mile wherever they can.

4. Fight Fair

The hallmark of a healthy relationship is the friction that occasionally erupts from equal partners rubbing each other the wrong way. In the homespace and the workplace, disagreements will flare. Temperatures will be raised. People will reach an impasse. Someone will become indignant that someone else has done something they consider wrong, stupid, or inconsiderate. Someone else will feel hurt, insulted, or disrespected. There will be hostilities, some passing and some permanent, depending on how the conflict is resolved.

Even when the partners to a disagreement are equal, situations may favour one over the other. Inevitably, one party has access to superior information or resources. They have more time, more money, or more leverage. My client Jim was recently involved in a negotiation with his holding company. After twenty years of partnership, he and his management team believed that their personal equity stake in the joint venture should be raised. His holding company ownership turned down his request and threatened to renegotiate terms of agreement that would make life difficult for Jim and his team. It was a clear demonstration of hardball tactics that stopped Jim and his team in their tracks. Jim conceded his request, but with a huge sense of personal injury. He was gobsmacked by their recalcitrance. He and his team are now actively involved in shopping their services to another partner.

So what makes a fight fair? First, you must know when to fight. Then, you must know how to fight. You have to pick the right time, place, and issue. You need to be sure it's worthwhile because a fight usually requires you to expend more energy and effort, and can impact emotional and financial resources.

If your side has the upper hand, you need to balance any short-term gains with the longer-term damage your win could cause to the relationship. You don't want to win the battle only to lose the war. Being satisfied with less could pay dividends in the longer term. Preserving the other side's sense of dignity and agency is paramount.

On the other hand, will the potential upside of winning outweigh the potential downside of losing the fight? You need to anticipate your actions if the decision goes against you. How far are you willing to go? Can you live with a losing outcome? Are you doing the best thing for your constituents?

A sign of relational health is to effectively use the lessons from the conflict resolution to prevent future conflict. Every relationship is a source of learning, but did the conflict provoke you to learn the right lessons, or did it simply reinforce flawed ways of thinking? This requires sober reflection: What was the conflict return on investment and was it worth it? That's why talking and, more critically, listening, is so important—you get others' perspective in real time, which can serve to clarify or challenge your own thinking.

In the personal space, the number one reason why couples fight is nothing. That's right—nothing! It begins as a disagreement over something as trivial as what program to watch or where to go to dinner. Then it expands into a broader issue, which is probably the reason for the conflict in the first place. If everything was copacetic, the argument wouldn't have happened. Once it starts, all it takes is the phrase "you always..." or "you never..." or "if you would just allow me to finish..." or "if you would only listen..." According to John Gottman, the Einstein of love, what matters is not the fight itself, and especially not what it is about, but how partners respond to negative emotions in the relationship. If couples see the conflict as an opportunity for growth, they can attune to each other and increase their understanding of one another, which deepens their trust in each other and in the relationship.

Be aware of your goals in the conversation. Your phrases are a means to an end. They can be slapdowns (If you would just let me finish...) or they can be lift-ups (I feel heard by you). If you make it a dance, rather than a fight, the result will always be more agreeable to both parties. Here are the phrases that can turn the experience from a fight into a dance:

- Yes and . . .
- I see your point of view . . .
- I hear you . . .
- I understand . . .
- I appreciate . . .
- I'm sorry for . . .
- I got it wrong . . .
- I shouldn't have . . .
- That's right . . .
- I acknowledge you . . .

5. Clarify and Contractualize Mutual Commitments

The road to relationship breakdowns is paved with ambiguity. Without clear expectations that have been written down and agreed to by all parties, uncertainty and confusion are sure to follow. The phrases that nobody wants to hear are: "I thought you said you were going to do that" or "Wasn't that your responsibility?" or "I expected you to handle that." The ensuing conversations are filled with blame, upset, and frustration. At best, they can be quickly resolved. At worst, they erode trust and mutual understanding.

Formal deals, employment contracts, and legal arrangements have written agreements that are signed by all parties. Healthy relationships require the same rigour and governance. Every project or venture should be carefully articulated. A handshake is a good starting point, but it must be papered. Key meetings should always be followed by a recording of what was discussed and agreed on. Whoever takes the minutes controls what was actually said. They don't need to be elaborate—just a concise expression of the accountabilities and timing. Fortunately, many virtual meeting programs allow for audio recording, so long as everyone consents.

Nothing says you're serious about follow-through like accurately stating your commitments and owning next steps. Then you need to honour your word while you hold others accountable to theirs.

A client of mine reframed his relationship with his wife by drawing up a one-page contract of how they would move forward together, based on a heart-to-heart conversation. They pinned the contract to the fridge so they would see it multiple times a day. Violating it is not an option for either person. It's reinvigorated their partnership and love for each other.

6. Own Everyone's Success but Accept Their Failures

It may take two to tango, but one dancer usually cares more about the outcome. In every relationship, one party cares more than the other(s) about the success of certain situations. Sales cares more about sales. Finance cares more about finance. IT cares more about IT. Ultimate success happens when someone cares more about it *all*.

The people who care more about it all are the Extra Milers. They take personal ownership for the success of the collective. They transcend their job description to include responsibility for the performance of their colleagues and even their customers. They consider their job description table stakes. They play a bigger game. People like this represent less than 5 percent of all employees but they account for over a third of all value-added collaborations (collaborations that require people to go above and beyond their job descriptions). They are the heart and soul of the organizations they serve.

These Extra Milers have unreasonable expectations of themselves. They take responsibility for enabling everyone in their orbit to reach their goals. You may be one of them, which is probably why you're reading this book. You want to expand your capacity to help others achieve even more. You pursue service over self-interest. Your need for credit and acknowledgement is far less important than great results—through collaborative relationships—which serve the common good.

Extra Milers bring out the best in their stakeholders. Somehow, they create synergies and co-operation that deliver remarkable outcomes. That's what drives them. Their dopamine centers are set off by the outperformance of their communities. They lead from the front. All the fatigue and frustrations are worthwhile because they pale in comparison to the big score.

What makes Extra Milers truly special is that they don't blame others for underperformance. They consider themselves 100 percent responsible. They do what they can and let go of what they can't. Extra Milers are as interested in the welfare of others as they are in their own. They don't point fingers, they lock arms.

THE QUICK WIN

Diane views her relationships with her team members as the most critical factor in her venture's success. She says, "Even more than financing and executive support, which are incredibly important and valuable, if my team members don't believe my relationship with them is authentic—if I don't follow every one of our six rules for relationship health—I'm toast. They're the ones who are building my dream: writing the code, getting the word out, making sure it's safe and it works really well. We can have conflict and mess up on communication, but I must show up with a smile, lift everyone up, own the mistakes and fight for the win. And the best part is the reward for nurturing these relationships—I love what I'm doing, I love my team, and we're changing the world!"

Review your personal rules for relationship health. See if they align with the six rules we've laid out. This isn't an easy task—it requires thoughtful and honest reflection. Be willing to adjust, subtract, or add the rules that will maximize your relationship health. Decide whether your rules are the same for the workplace as the homespace. Ask yourself how they would differ and why.

5

Understand the Art and Neuroscience of Conflict Resolution

DIANE IS A SCIENCE JUNKIE. She says, "It makes me feel more in control of my own thoughts, feelings, and behaviours when I understand what's actually happening, at a microscopic level, inside my brain and body when I'm dealing with stress. Admittedly, that's my thing, but I think it's important to share this information so people don't just think of themselves as weak, ineffective, or hopeless. For me, there's something empowering and hopeful about knowing how my brain works and how I can actually change and become more effective, no matter how old I am, if that's what I want to do."

Conflict is like electricity—very little happens without it. It becomes more intense the closer you come to achieving a breakthrough. Often, the intensity of the conflict is directly related to the size of change you are trying to create. It may be a serious disagreement with others, a fundamental difference of perspective, or a private confusion about what course of action to take. It's always difficult, and often painful. By definition, there's no simple way to resolve it, instantly or easily. If there was, it wouldn't be a conflict. It would just be a clarification.

Conflict is the enemy of safety. Resolving conflict is the essence of safety. Healthy cultures create a space for opposing points of view to be stated and shared openly. It's called constructive dissent—the encouragement to express one's opinion and challenge the status quo as a matter of course. There will always be tension in this kind of exchange, especially when the stakes are high and people are invested in their desired outcomes. But feeling like You Belong Here is motivation to navigate the tension in pursuit of a common goal or mission.

When conflict is resolved successfully, it fosters a sense of belonging. When it's neglected or mismanaged, it festers until there's an inevitable eruption. That's a disproportionate response, an angry outburst, or the departure of talent. Even worse, it can fracture the company or community. Prolonged conflicts can cause irreparable harm.

Most brains experience conflict as a crisis, meaning something that must be managed quickly because conflict creates stress. It's necessary to understand what stress is and how severe, prolonged stress negatively impacts our mental health. For example, when you are out for a walk, everything your senses experience is transmitted to your thalamus, the brain structure that gathers information from everything you see, hear, taste, or touch. If, during the walk, you are suddenly confronted by a growling dog with its teeth bared, the instant you see and hear the dog, that sensory information will go directly from your thalamus to your amygdala. The amygdala, the brain structure that receives sensory information related to threatening situations at lightning speed, instantly considers the information and develops a plan: freeze, flee, or fight.

In response to a threatening event, the amygdala forwards fear-related messages to the brain's stress response command center, called the hypothalamic-pituitary-adrenal axis (HPAA). The hypothalamus is a brain structure that controls many essential functions necessary for life, including maintaining our circadian rhythm (normal sleep and wake cycles) and regulating hormone levels, appetite, body temperature, sexual behaviour, and emotions. The hypothalamus is located close to and works closely with the pituitary gland, which produces essential hormones that regulate the thyroid, sexual functioning, and stress responses.

The message sent from the amygdala in response to that aggressive dog would request a burst of the neurotransmitter norepinephrine, which increases your heart and breathing rate and blood pressure, allowing you to run or take other evasive measures. The amygdala would also ask the hypothalamus to release corticotropin-releasing hormone (CRH), which initiates a cascade of effects when we are exposed to an anxiety-provoking situation. CRH prompts the pituitary gland to release adrenocorticotropic hormone (ACTH), and ACTH triggers the release of cortisol, our most important stress hormone.

Cortisol is a potent anti-inflammatory hormone. Its job is to manage our body's response to stress and calm us down as quickly as possible, to prevent widespread tissue and nerve damage associated with stress and inflammation—

I'll be talking much more about inflammation and physical and mental health in chapter 9. In response to a threat, a boost of cortisol is necessary to provide the energy needed to mount an effective response that keeps us alive and well. Once there is enough cortisol to calm the brain and the body, an "all clear" message is sent to the hypothalamus, which turns off the CRH tap until it's required again. In the short term, the stress-induced increase in cortisol is crucial and even life-saving. It prepares you to face the threat, but it's not necessarily conducive to resolving conflict with others.

What's the Win Here?

The conflict-resolution hormones are a cocktail of dopamine, oxytocin, and endorphins. Dopamine is known as the "feel-good" hormone. It gives you a sense of pleasure and satisfaction. It's part of your reward system that encourages you to seek even more of those positive feelings. Dopamine is a highly effective motivator when it's linked to the right behaviours. It can also be addictive. Junk food and sugar trigger the release of dopamine, which makes you want to consume even more of them.

By framing conflict resolution as a reward to be pursued, not a crisis to be endured, you can convert the process into an activity that relaxes people and stimulates their dopamine production. This requires constant acknowledgement and celebration of each small step along the way. That's why Diane's favourite question is "What's the win here?" Winning is a major generator of dopamine. By focusing people on the win, you open the spigots of dopamine.

Oxytocin is known as the bonding hormone. It is released when we feel a strong connection to the people around us.

It's a basic building block of trust and affection. It can be stimulated through a simple phrase of rapport or a gesture like shaking hands, hugging, or a pat on the back. We've all experienced those wonderful moments when we click with the people around us and cross the threshold of conflict into co-operation and collaboration. By expressing our connection with the people around us, we can accelerate and multiply those moments.

Endorphins are chemicals released during pleasurable activities such as exercise, massage, eating, and sex. They are also released by enjoyable conversations, laughing, recognition, and kudos. They help relieve pain, reduce stress, and improve overall sense of well-being. By continually focusing on the contribution and progress made by others, you can enhance the production of endorphins—and create an environment that strengthens peoples' desire to find solutions.

It's important to remember that your sensations (e.g., what you see, hear, and touch) and your thoughts and feelings create neurochemical changes in your body that can empower or disempower you to play at your best. By consciously reframing an activity from something to be evaded to something to be embraced, you can physically enable yourself to perform it more effectively. Unlike the Hulk, who unleashes his superpower when he's enraged and flooded with cortisol, you will unleash your superpowers when you turn on your endorphins, dopamine, and oxytocin.

Mike and Diane's Intentional Steps to Resolving Conflict

In a way, all of life is about conflict resolution—both big and small. On any given day, you'll be called upon to remove obstacles, solve problems, and bring people together. Diane and I literally make a living by helping people resolve conflicts—both private and public. Here are the intentional steps we've learned to take:

1. Always begin with the best possible outcome in mind—a win for everyone.
2. Fully understand the context of the conversation or negotiation.
3. Find common ground—articulate the win in a way that is embraced by all parties.
4. Speak less, listen more. Make sure each party feels heard.
5. Keep expressing the belief that the issues will be resolved. Reiterate your commitment to the win.
6. Be true to your values while you encourage others to stay true to theirs. Ensure that others know your values and you know theirs.
7. Deconstruct the main issue into smaller steps and take them one at a time.
8. Look for the sticking points—people will get stuck on minor things that they believe are major. Acknowledge the significance of these points to them and express your determination to resolve them.
9. Believe that people can change throughout the process if you present the options in an appropriate manner.
10. Manage the tension—treat eruptions as expressions of fear to be assuaged. Demonstrate your understanding of the issues behind the issues. Show kindness and empathy with others' concerns or doubts.

11. Beware of hyperbole—it's inflammatory. If you hear it, immediately work to cool it down.
12. Articulate the other party's stance in such a way that they reply, "That's right."
13. Know when to stop and take a break. Regroup and come back. Don't leave it hanging. Get it dealt with in an appropriate time frame. Become known as someone who closes the loop.
14. Own the responsibility for finding a solution. Be the agent of resolution.
15. If it becomes clear there is no runway, call in a third party to mediate the solution.
16. Know that you will make mistakes. Getting things wrong isn't wrong, it's inevitable. What counts is what you do afterwards to make it right.

On an interpersonal level, conflict with a spouse, friend, or co-worker is usually much more personal, which can sometimes make resolution more challenging. Too often, we hear what we want to hear, make up stories in our mind to support that narrative, and fail to express how we feel or what we need in a mature, measured manner. Marriages end, friends drift apart, and employees move on if these conflicts aren't navigated skillfully. Communication is key—instead of clamming up, consider following these four critical steps:

1. Tell the person what you thought you heard or experienced. Avoid "You said" and try "I heard..." or "I thought..." Acknowledge you might have misunderstood or misheard (unless there's a court stenographer, that's more likely than not). This shows them you're seeking a

resolution. Keep it short, tight, and as emotionless as possible, such as, "I thought you were ignoring me."

2. Share what you decided, based on what you thought or heard. For instance, "I decided you were taking me for granted because I thought you were purposely ignoring me." Acknowledging you could be misinterpreting the situation gives the other person an opportunity to see how you might have come to that conclusion. Your vulnerability is an important salve for difficult communication.

3. Tell them how you feel (briefly): "My assumption made me feel sad."

4. Tell them what you need (again, be brief). For example, "I would appreciate your putting down your phone when I'm speaking to you." The other person will be less likely to take a defensive stance if you give them a clear idea of the problem and a path ahead.

6

Know That without the Yin, the Yang Will Crash and Burn

MEN AND WOMEN ARE DIFFERENT. Duh! Genetically, males are more like other males (99.9 percent) than they are similar to females (98.5 percent), which is the same percentage similarity human males share with chimpanzees (98.5 percent). (Note that every person is unique, so writing about these differences necessarily requires generalizations, which aren't applicable to every man and every woman.) The often dramatic disparity in response to life's extreme moments by gender is therefore no surprise, but it is still widely misunderstood. We are talking about averages and overlapping ranges, after all—and we still have very little data for people who are gender non-conforming. But according to large-scale studies documented in *Scientific American*, there are significant differences between the typical male and female personality profiles.

On average, males tend to be more dominant, assertive, risk-prone, thrill-seeking, tough-minded, emotionally stable, utilitarian, and open to abstract ideas. Males also tend to score higher on self-estimates of intelligence, even though sex differences in general intelligence—measured as an ability—are negligible. Men also tend to form larger, competitive groups in which hierarchies tend to be stable and in which individual relationships tend to require little emotional investment. In terms of communication style, males tend to use more assertive speech and are more likely to interrupt people (both men and women) more often—especially *intrusive* interruptions—which can be interpreted as a form of dominant behaviour.

In contrast, females, *on average*, tend to be more sociable, sensitive, warm, compassionate, polite, anxious, self-doubting, and more open to aesthetics. *On average*, women are more interested in intimate, co-operative dyadic relationships that are more emotion focused and characterized by unstable hierarchies and strong egalitarian norms. If aggression does arise, it tends to be more indirect and less openly confrontational. Females also tend to have better communication skills, displaying higher verbal ability, and are more able to decode other people's non-verbal behaviour. Women also tend to use more affiliative and tentative speech in their language and be more expressive, both through facial expressions and body language (men, however, tend to adopt a more expansive, open posture).

In addition to sex-related differences associated with the risk of developing depression, large population research has indicated that men and women tend to experience different depression or anxiety symptoms and may respond differently to treatments. Women seem to be more likely to have classic or internalizing depression symptoms like sadness, anhedonia (lack of pleasure), anxiety, physical symptoms, and reversed vegetative symptoms, such as increased appetite and weight gain. Conversely, men may be more likely to experience externalizing symptoms, such as irritability and anger, as well as substance abuse and other addictive behaviours. In general, men tend to react more strongly to stress associated with failure and a lack of expected achievement, while women tend to react more strongly to stress associated with rejection or conflict.

Additionally, women are also more likely to experience marital/relationship discord when depressed, while men may report more problems at work. Interestingly, research has demonstrated that men tend to have a stronger physiological response to stress than women. This means that their brains and bodies react more powerfully to stress, by releasing higher levels of stress hormones, experiencing greater increases in heart rate and blood pressure, and feeling more negative emotions or more feelings of aggression.

If you look closely, the research shows that there are *way* more women than men who are super-agreeable and *way* more men than women who are super-disagreeable. Women are, on average, better than men at forming relationships. They are ecosystem builders. They are more likely to meet other like-minded people and be more social. They are the social planners and the connectors. That's why men do best when they're married. Without their wives, they struggle to integrate themselves into their communities.

And all of this is why we need good gender diversity in workplaces: to even out the imbalances, to draw on the strengths and help address the weaknesses of each side. A major 2020 McKinsey research study examined a data set of more than a thousand large companies in fifteen countries and found that companies in the top quartile for gender diversity were 25 percent more likely to have above-average profitability than companies in the fourth quartile. Companies in the top quartile of ethnic and cultural diversity were 36 percent more likely to outperform on profitability. The highest-performing companies on both profitability and diversity had more women in line roles (that is, owning a line of business) than in staff roles on their executive teams. The research also found a penalty for bottom-quartile performance on gender diversity: companies in the bottom quartile for both gender and ethnic diversity were 27 percent more likely to underperform the industry average than all other firms.

National governments and corporate leadership need to advance the cause of gender and ethnic diversity, but individuals must also contribute, from advocating for themselves in their own careers to helping others advance through sponsorship and mentorship. At work, they can be proactive in supporting diversity, speaking up if they see inappropriate behaviours, and fostering an environment where education regarding diversity is encouraged.

10 Things That Can Help Navigate the Differences between Men and Women

So what does this mean in plain, actionable terms? Leaders who understand that men and women may approach challenges, conflicts, and relationships quite differently are better equipped to build a more compassionate, inclusive, collaborative workplace. Here are the ten things that can help you navigate the differences between men and women. Share them, get feedback, and learn from your own experiences:

1. Men tend to be drawn more to the bright, shiny, and new. Women are often more cognizant of the risk. Together, they achieve balance.

2. Men tend to focus more on the task and outcome. Women focus more on the process and effective collaboration. Together, they achieve equilibrium.

3. Women are more apt to organize and administer the moving parts behind the curtain. Men are more likely to crave the glory and kudos that come from leading the charge. We need to stop seeing women as the gender that just gets the team to opening day. They need to be front and center with men.

4. Men more often go with their gut, while women are more rigorously analytical. It's not about women's intuition—it's about women's analytics. A team needs to consider both gut feel and analytical acumen, not necessarily in equal measure, when determining strategy.

5. Women tend to be more consensus oriented, while men lean toward making the decision. Their complementary styles can produce optimal results.

6. Men tend to be more assertive and are more likely to interrupt. Women are more apt to listen and co-pilot their way forward with others. Many women benefit from building their assertiveness muscle, and men need to listen.

7. Women are often more attuned to the social dynamics of the group. They understand the informal network of leaders and influencers. Men tend toward hierarchical structures. Working together, they maximize the functionality of the collective.

8. Women are often more patient and thorough. Men tend to rush toward completion. Together, they need to find the prudent middle path.

9. Men tend to be uncomfortable talking about their feelings. Women understand the power of cathartic conversations that address emotions. Men need to confront their inhibitions while women make it safe for them to do so.

10. Women are wary (and very tired) of misogyny. Men are afraid of doing or saying the wrong thing. Together, they need to create workplaces that foster effective communication and ensure everyone is treated with respect.

THE QUICK WIN

Diane and I have frequently discussed the dynamics and differences between men and women, with Diane always prefacing her comments with, "We need to be careful not to paint all men or all women with a broad brush." After hearing that repeatedly, I asked her why this seemed so important to her. She shared, "My first foray into the corporate world showed me that men and women can be equally wonderful and equally awful. I do believe men and women often approach the world differently, but I try to see everyone as a whole, not as their gender. That said, I have loved working with some incredible women who are assertive, have rock-solid boundaries, and are driven to win, which are often seen as 'male' characteristics, while at the same time, being gentle, collaborative, compassionate, and generous. Vive la difference!"

In the next appropriate moment, when a "gender situation" arises, consider sharing your reasons for responding as you did. If you feel like you aren't achieving the desired level of rapport and safety, ask for guidance to improve your outcomes. Ask the other people present for their reasons. If that doesn't seem appropriate, share with a small group of trusted but gender-diverse friends or associates. Sometimes we aren't aware of our own biases or ingrained behaviours and how they might be experienced by others. Become known as someone who actively seeks to see things with others' perspectives.

I

Creating Belonging in a Hybrid World

II

Growing Enriching Relationships

III

Owning Your Power

IV

Winning on the Brink

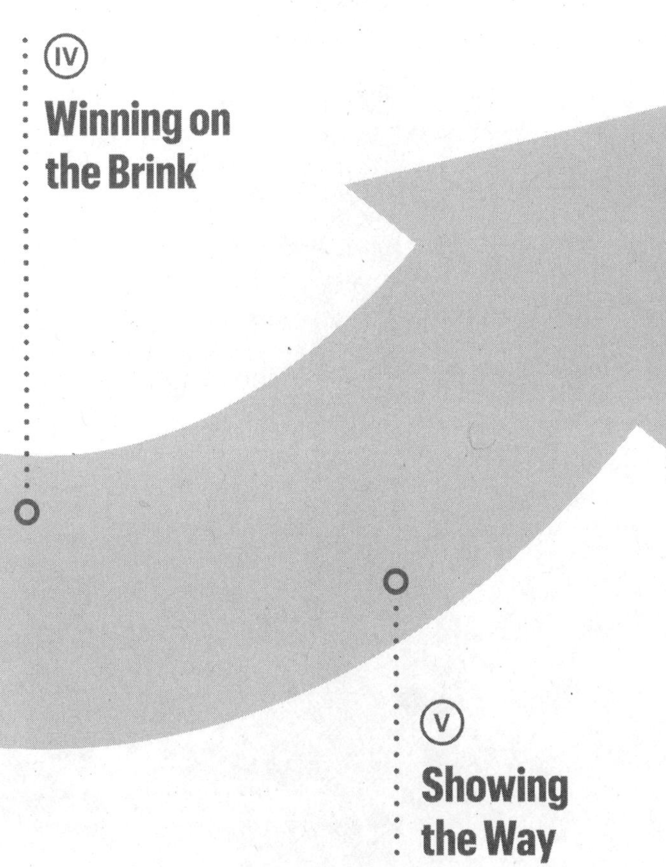

V

Showing the Way

PART III

OWNING YOUR POWER

7

Accept That the Only Person You Can Control Is You

ON JULY 8, 2022, the Canadian telecom provider Rogers Communications experienced a major service outage affecting more than twelve million internet and cellular network users, including me. That morning I had planned a long-awaited Zoom call with a team of senior prospects on a major new coaching contract. The problem was that they lived in America and they had no idea about the outage. I felt the frustration and impotence of being stymied by events beyond my control. My upset was exacerbated by a text I received from the lead client when I retrieved it five hours later, after the network was back up: "The team logged on to our call this morning, but you didn't show up. What's up?"

Even though I explained the situation the following morning, I was chagrined that the prospect felt like they were ghosted. Diane experienced similar emotions when she missed a Zoom meeting with me because she had just succumbed to COVID. She apologized so profusely that I felt guilty for even following up with her. "To me," Diane said, "someone else's time is valuable, so I am embarrassed when I make my patients, or anyone else, wait. I run on time. If I'm late, I'm breaking my own code and that's unacceptable to me. It's disrespectful to others."

The situations become much more serious when you feel like you're being intentionally diminished by others. We're all confronting a future that threatens to overwhelm us. When we believe we're being disrespected by others, it reminds us of how puny we really are. It's just another deposit in our insignificance account. On the other hand, when we're celebrated or recognized, we feel rejuvenated. We want to do more and bring more to that relationship. Getting kudos is highly addictive. While it's not always healthy, the fact is that the way other people treat us ultimately impacts how we view ourselves.

I work with a client who is a senior executive at a financial services company. He is a gentle, soft-spoken man in his late forties. He works for a forceful, narcissistic boss who continually accuses him of not "pulling his weight" and being a "serial disappointer." It takes my client weeks to recover from these meetings. He retreats into a shell and stays there. He would like to leave but the financial sacrifice is too high for him. My guidance to him is to detach himself emotionally from the meeting and observe the scenario as if from a distance. With this perspective, he can see that his boss behaves like this with everyone. My client can also see that his boss is highly effective in areas where he is not. He can now endure the meetings by viewing them as the price of doing business. At some point, he may decide that the price is too high and move on.

Be Brave

Diane has had many patients who have spent their lives trying to make the difficult or negative people around them change. Her message to them is always the same: the only person on earth you can control is *you*. That simple fact is often easily acknowledged but rarely deeply embraced, but in Diane's mind, "It's freeing. Once you truly accept that you have no control over anyone else—not your partner, child, boss, co-worker, or parent—you are then free to stop trying to exert control. More importantly, you can shift your energy toward recognizing and amplifying the control you do have, over your own thoughts, feelings, and behaviours. This is the central pillar of personal well-being. If you don't feel like you have control of yourself, you'll feel anxious and awful. That's when you can really benefit from speaking to a trained therapist."

It's easy to relinquish your power to bullies and narcissists, because they can appear formidable and larger than life. They are the people that brand others as idiots and losers. They apply such unkind labels to diminish and minimize. Even when they're confronted with irrefutable evidence and trackable truths, they'll deny it. They know they're wrong, but they attack others as a means of defending themselves. They may believe that they are better than anyone else (narcissists) or wish they were (bullies), but their actions are fear based.

A narcissist is someone who has an inflated sense of self-importance and believes they are entitled to favourable treatment and immediate compliance with their demands. They exaggerate their accomplishments and view themselves as being special, unique and better than others. They lack empathy and crave admiration and attention, often exploiting others to get what they want. Narcissists are often terrible bullies, but not all bullies are narcissists. A bully is someone who attempts to intimidate or dominate others by being physically, verbally, or emotionally aggressive. Unlike narcissists, some bullies don't have an inflated sense of self-worth. In fact, they feel quite inferior, so they target those who they perceive as weaker or vulnerable, which makes them feel more powerful and in control.

Most of us have had people in our lives who trigger feelings of almost childlike helplessness or rage. You need to be aware and courageous enough to stand tall and push back. Narcissists and bullies do not want to be directly attacked, but they also (secretly) respect strength. You must be unyielding on boundaries and what is acceptable, and avoid lowering yourself to the same level. They want you to get down into the mud with them. Rise above that. It's about being impersonal when the other person is making it much too personal. You can be respectful and direct at the same time. No matter how great your fear, you can protect yourself by always being true to your values—these are the lines that you will not cross. Three very dangerous words, when spoken together, are "just this once."

It's critical to know that a true narcissist, believing they are important, entitled, and special, and that you are not, will hit back on any and all criticism, ten-fold. That's also called narcissistic rage, which is a hair-trigger, disproportionate response to even a perceived slight. The level of hostility, rage, or resentment is always so out of proportion to the provocation that others are shocked by the over-the-top response.

Diane's mantra is "Be brave"—push past the inner kid who is probably being activated by past humiliations or traumas. Diane shares that when she's really frustrated, instead of behaving in an angry manner, shouting and being defensive, she becomes tearful, and that drives her crazy. She *hates* it. People can interpret a tearful woman as being manipulative or volatile—trying to control or dominate the situation. But that's how Diane expresses her anger. She cries when she is angry or frustrated. She gets bruises on her arms from pinching herself to deflect her attention from crying and just breathe. She can see people thinking that she's pulling the girl card. That's a big challenge for women, particularly in the business world.

At a recent meeting of prominent psychiatrists, Diane and a female colleague, the only women in the group, found themselves being "mansplained" to by a male colleague. He spoke down to both of them, clearly unaware of his condescension or the offence he was causing. Diane was very clear that she fully understood the issue and, with a slight edge in her voice, subtly suggested that her male colleague refrain from over-elaborating these points in the future. The other men at the table looked mortified, with downcast eyes or pleading looks of apology. By asserting herself in the moment, strongly and directly, without emotion or condescension, she held the power in the room and achieved a successful outcome. Her male colleague might not change, because she can't control him, but she didn't allow his belittling behaviour to stand and become an acceptable narrative.

When a woman starts to emote in a meeting, I don't understand the source of those tears. All I understand is that a crisis is unfolding. I'm out of my depth. I'm uncomfortable. I'm also afraid that I caused the tears so I'm going to be culpable in some way. I'm also surprised when strong women cry

Small things make or break trust. In other words, there are no such things as small things.

because I misinterpret it as a sign of weakness. I want to step in and rescue her or somehow provide a solution.

Meanwhile, Diane is thinking, "How dare you!?" Her anger or frustration presents itself as tears. So, the way she has positioned her response in her mind is that vulnerability is a leadership superpower. It gives her strength. She actually puts words to her behaviour by saying, "I feel ridiculous right now because this emotion is reflecting my frustration at this conversation. I am not sad. I am frustrated." She translates what her behaviour should mean to others. That enables them to respond appropriately. She also turns it into humour by saying, for example, "No one is allowed to take a selfie with me right now." Once she laughs, she's OK to continue.

My way of reacting to acute anger or frustration is to tighten up from the inside out. I start to breathe fast and shallow. I lose my inner clarity. I stutter. I feel a sense of indignation that can be crippling. My words come out in a disjointed rush. Even as I'm speaking, I'm aware of how little sense I'm making. That's my visceral signal to regather my wits about me, pause, center myself, and carry on. I acknowledge that my dysfunction is a response to the emotions created by the moment; so that others can comprehend why I'm behaving that way, I will say, "When I heard you say... I felt... that's why I reacted like..." It enables others to empathize with me. Often, they will reveal that they had no intention to make me feel that way. A clearing is created to resolve the issue.

Research shows that when one person shares personal details in a conversation, the other person typically responds in kind. Psychologists call this *mutual self-disclosure*, and studies show it helps people feel closer to one another. You don't even have to share intimacies. Start by talking about something you're excited about, or fear, or are concerned about.

Make the Invisible Visible

The reason you can't control anyone but yourself is because you never know what is really, truly going on in someone else's brain or in their life, unless they tell you, truthfully. People in horrifying circumstances are able to lie to their captors and make them believe their lies, to keep themselves alive. Anyone who believes they are exerting full control over another person would be shocked to learn that they are fighting a losing battle—you cannot own another person's thoughts and feelings. You must earn their love, respect, and positive feelings.

All of us are fighting battles that no one knows anything about until they show themselves in our actions. Even then, others might know we're not ourselves, but they don't know why. Our past is embedded deep in our psyches. We respond to our interpretation of the situation, not the situation itself. There is no such thing as an objective view of reality. Being aware of our kryptonite, the situations that make us feel weak, overwhelmed, or ineffective, is a major step toward being able to master them. By creating the space for people to share what they're going through, or what they've been through, we make it easier for them to deal with their kryptonite. For example, we could simply ask, "Are you able to tell me what's going on so we can work through it together?" or "I see you're not OK with this. Can you tell me why?"

If there is an expressed emotion, it can be dealt with. But if people keep their feelings buried, it's harder for others to help them. The key is to make the invisible visible, without feeling that your self-transparency will compromise you or alienate others. This is perhaps why the suicide rate is highest for middle-aged white men. They turn their anger inward. They don't share how they're feeling. Women may have twice the rate of depression and anxiety and make more attempts to kill themselves, but men are almost four times more likely to end their life by suicide, by using more lethal means, compared to women. Keeping it all inside bakes in the painful thoughts that come with depression: worthlessness, uselessness, and hopelessness.

How you respond to difficult or disappointing situations defines you in the eyes of others, especially when the relationship is new. It's how you show your cards. Small things make or break others' trust in you. In other words, there are no such things as small things. For example, simply acknowledging that what is important to others is also important to you magnifies their connection to you. Making time to listen, and truly listening, or following up exactly as you said you would, are small but critical behaviours that build trust. The more certain they become of your commitment and consistency toward them, the greater their level of faith in you. In every meeting, you train people how to expect you to be in the next meeting. Ultimately, those expectations become self-fulfilling. Diane and I want people to know that we will always be all-in in every conversation, no matter what else is going on in our lives. It's literally how we make a living.

THE QUICK WIN

In this chapter, I shared how both Diane and I react to anger and frustration, even in important business meetings, and how we've worked to manage those emotional responses.

Take some time to identify how you react to personal or professional frustration. It might help to ask someone you trust, as we don't always see ourselves as others do. Try to get granular: consider not just how you are feeling (frustrated/angry), but also what you're thinking when you feel that way ("I'm being a loser" or "I want to hit someone") and how you behave (scary face, massaging temple, head shaking dismissively). Then you need to ask yourself whether you feel you can control those thoughts, feelings, and behaviours. If you have a momentary transgression, but you can quickly recover your sense of self-control, that's completely normal. We are human. But if you identify a pattern of feeling "out of control"—acting, speaking, and/or feeling in a manner that you can't control—you might benefit from some professional guidance.

8

Realize That You Have a Remarkable Capacity for Change

HUMAN BEINGS HAVE a remarkable capacity for change. A leopard may not be able to change its spots, but people are not leopards. Sixty years of combined experience at the most extreme level have shown Diane and me how dramatically people can recreate themselves, learning new ways of thinking and behaving that benefit them and those around them. The question is not whether you can change, it's how much you really want to change, and if you're willing to do the work.

The worst kind of lies are the ones that we tell ourselves. When we don't honour the data, when we ignore the science, and refuse to listen to our instincts, we are actively deceiving ourselves. Either as an individual or as a group, we can be dominated by what we want to believe, even though every sign points in a different direction. We could call it the *autocrat media strategy*: tell your citizens they're not seeing what they're actually seeing. Diane calls it crazy-making, or she says with her innate candour, "Don't piss on my leg and tell me it's raining." It's commonly referred to as gaslighting. When you are confronted with a person who tells you that what you know to be true is not, it's time to head for the exit. You cannot communicate or negotiate with them.

There is a fine balance between listening to our gut and transcending unconscious bias. That's when we need to confer with others. Sometimes, it takes a village to discern the truth in a situation and find the best path forward. We need to be open, but not naive. We cannot operate on automatic pilot. We need a diverse personal board of directors that we can consult, especially on matters that have a broad range of potential impacts. Diane is on my personal board of directors, along with a range of people that I thank in the Acknowledgements section of this book. A constellation of C-suite clients from companies around the world also provide me with a view of how their companies are mastering change. Media like the *New York Times*, *Wall Street Journal*, *Fast Company*, the *Economist*, and CNBC further enrich my perspective. As I wrote this book, I did even more research and had even more conversations with experts. It's a never-ending smorgasbord of insights that enable me to reach the most balanced decisions in the face of accelerating change.

Expanding your capacity for change is a 12/6 (that's twelve hours a day, six days a week) endeavour—you also need time to switch off and internalize the data. But it's not onerous if you're curious and love to learn.

Good Neuroplasticity versus Bad Neuroplasticity

As Diane shared in *This Is Depression*, human beings can grow new neurons throughout their life. Growing new neurons is called neurogenesis. It occurs in a few brain regions but especially in the hippocampus. Not only can we grow new brain cells, we can also change our brain in another remarkable way. The human brain is constantly wiring and rewiring in response to influences like learning new information and developing new skills, engaging social interactions, and other enriching life experiences.

The brain's ability to remodel itself is called neuroplasticity. It can be good for you, but it can also perpetuate and entrench problems. Good neuroplasticity is when you learn a new skill—bike riding, dancing, or learning to read a room. Every skill requires practice to establish new brain wiring. Neurons that fire together wire together, creating brain superhighways, which are the easiest paths for us to follow. Each time you practice, the wiring gets stronger and more efficient, and before long, you don't need to think about doing the new activity—it feels like it comes naturally. While neuroplasticity occurs throughout life, the brain is most plastic during childhood and adolescence, which is why it's faster and easier to learn a new language, swim, dance, or learn just about anything when we're young.

A compelling example of bad neuroplasticity is the repetitive behaviour associated with obsessive-compulsive disorder (OCD). People who struggle with OCD commonly have compulsive behaviours; for instance, they might feel compelled to check the stove to be sure that it's turned off. Unfortunately, they can't just check it once, feel reassured, and get on with their day; they might need to check it hundreds of times every day. While they might feel momentarily reassured when they check the stove, within moments the intrusive thought "the stove might be on" creeps back into their head, and they feel they must check it again. Compulsions are examples of bad neuroplasticity because OCD establishes very strong and long-lasting wiring, resulting from neurons firing together repeatedly: every time they check the stove, the wiring is further reinforced and strengthened.

The psychological treatment that has the most research evidence supporting its effectiveness for OCD is a type of cognitive-behavioural therapy (CBT) called exposure and response prevention (ERP). If our stove-checking friend was working with an excellent ERP therapist, they'd be taught to stand near the stove (exposure) but to try their best not to check the stove (response-prevention). As you might imagine, this is extremely difficult to do if they've been checking the stove hundreds of times every day. However, every time they don't check the stove, even though their brain is screaming, "CHECK THE STOVE!!!," they are rewiring their brain to say, "You don't need to check the stove." The good neuroplasticity of ERP can gradually undo the bad neuroplasticity of OCD compulsions.

Bad neuroplasticity also happens in depression. The more we think negative thoughts, the more likely we are to think and believe them. For example, if you say, "I'm so depressed," you can make a bad day the beginning of a negative thought spiral. That simple phrase can cause a slide into a mental abyss, leading to anxiety and helplessness. On the other hand, if you say "I feel down right now but I'll get over it," or "I'm having a depressing thought but I know it will pass quickly," you are building good neuroplasticity. If you can actually say "I'm struggling with this thought but I know rejecting it will make me stronger," you will embark on your own self-fulfilling journey.

Congratulate yourself whenever you replace a disempowering thought with an empowering one.

Whenever you catch yourself replacing a disempowering thought with an empowering one, congratulate yourself for mastering your mind in the moment. Throw yourself a micro-party that may be nothing more than a shout of triumph or a smile at yourself in the mirror. If you can share your triumph with others, it will be even more meaningful.

The same principle applies to obsessively checking texts, emails, Facebook, or Instagram. Every time you resist the gravitational pull of the incoming alert, celebrate your discipline. Get into the rhythm of rewarding yourself with social media indulgence after your deep work is finished.

And get into the habit of talking about the positive, not the negative. The way we speak to ourselves, our internal narrative, is a critical resilience tool—kind, empathic self-talk can promote mental health and wellness, while harsh, highly critical self-talk can undermine confidence and promote emotional distress. When we endlessly ruminate on negative thoughts or fears without shifting the focus to solutions, or when we fail to seek help if we're not able to find those solutions, the brain wiring that causes us to be negative and ruminate is reinforced. If you sit around and talk about your pain every day, your pain will worsen, and you will also be increasingly unpleasant company, which will push people away and continue the spiral. On the other hand, if you talk about healing, you will reduce the pain's severity, and you will encourage your community to help your recovery.

And remember: it's not all about you. We don't always know the full story behind someone's challenging behaviour—why are some bosses so cantankerous? Why is that salesperson so rude? They might not even know themselves why they've developed such an unpleasant internal and/or external narrative. Because we all should be working toward a more compassionate world, there's value to considering not just the person you see, but also the life of that person beyond what they've shown you. Maybe they just lost a loved one? Maybe they're being bullied? Maybe they're not feeling well? Give others the benefit of the doubt. You're here to be a Keeper of the Safety Flame and to create belonging, and one way you can do that is to contribute positively, not negatively, to their neuroplasticity—and to yours while you're doing it.

THE QUICK WIN

One of the most difficult things to do as a psychiatrist is to fire a patient. It's rarely happened in Diane's practice, because instances of her feeling unsafe or disrespected have been exceedingly rare. However, she reflected on the two times over twenty-five years that she had to end a therapeutic relationship before there was any real progress or recovery. "I can recall a couple of patients who were going through a difficult divorce and they only wanted to talk about how awful their soon-to-be ex was, all day, every day, to anyone who would listen. This included during every appointment we had, despite my efforts to explain why this was unhelpful to them (bad neuroplasticity), their children (exposing them to negativity about their other parent), and everyone around them, as their friends and family stopped calling. After countless appointments, I realized that I was not able to help them. It wasn't that they had an untreated mental illness that required intervention to break an obsessive thought pattern. They simply refused to believe that they were causing harm, and they were so angry and resentful, they didn't want to let those feelings go. So, I had to let them go, because I realized I was doing more work than they were."

Part of building good neuroplasticity is recognizing when you're building (or reinforcing) bad neuroplasticity. If you've been through a difficult time or you're currently struggling, try to slowly shift your focus away from feeling victimized and toward healing. Make it easier for your community to help you. Be aware of the kind of words that you're using. Get feedback from the people closest to you. And play the same role for them. This is sometimes not possible without professional help. Unlike Diane's example, where those patients didn't want to change their behaviours, if you want to change negative or destructive thoughts, feelings, and behaviours, you can with the right help. It's not easy, but it is definitely possible. As Diane always says to her patients when they're feeling hopeless, because she truly believes it, "There is *always* a path ahead."

9

Keep Body and Soul Together

WHEN YOU are taking care of your mind—your brain—you need to remember that your brain is part of your body, and the connection between your brain and the rest of your body matters a lot. Your life experiences can lead to important changes in how your brain is structured and how it functions and can critically impact your risk of mental and physical illness. The science explaining this connection is called epigenetics.

As Diane puts it in *This Is Depression*, think of DNA as like a piano keyboard. Every person has their own unique keyboard (except identical twins—they have identical keyboards), and each key represents a section of DNA known as a gene. The way the keys are played makes you who you are: the way specific genes are expressed (played) or suppressed (not played) directs what a cell will become. Specific genes make proteins and control traits like eye colour or height, and other genes direct cells to become heart, brain, or skin cells. Think of it as "your song" or "the music of you." Interestingly, your tune can change, and what causes that change is epigenetics.

Epigenetics is the science of gene expression: the interface between nature (the genes you inherited from your parents) and nurture (your life experiences). If you're lucky, you were raised in a family that invested you with a deep sense of self-worth and personal power. You were enveloped in an environment of love, warmth, and acceptance. Your home was a place of regeneration and safety and a refuge from the ups and downs of the external world. And if those statements described you, you're in the minority.

In fact, according to recent statistics, 70 percent to 80 percent of Americans consider their families dysfunctional. One in five Americans report they have been sexually molested; one in four grew up with one or more parents who drank too much; one in three couples have engaged in physical violence. Too many of us grow up in homes where we experienced abuse, chaos, or neglect.

These childhood experiences can powerfully shape your future because they may directly impact your biology. If you come from a family where abuse, or even neglect, was present, you're at risk. While a single devastating event can imprint itself on your life forever, more often it's chronic, repetitive traumas that accumulate, resulting in important health impacts. In short, our earliest memories can be our most lasting ones. As William Shakespeare wrote in *The Merchant of Venice*, "The sins of the father are to be laid upon the children."

I don't share these insights to alarm you. On the contrary, I share them to inform you, because I believe that with this knowledge comes power. I know. I grew up in a household wracked by extreme, violent outbursts. My father was disabled and died of heart disease at forty-two. My mother was a volatile artist who barely managed to financially support her family. She expressed her distress by cursing the world and severely, often physically, censuring my actions. I developed a fear of being wrong or being judged, especially by authority figures. I became an inveterate people pleaser, desperate for others' approval—even when it was never going to be forthcoming. I experienced clinical depression in my thirties and forties. Even now, as I head into my sixties, I need to be vigilant against the ever-present danger of going back down again. However, I've learned how to change my tune through my life experiences. I'm living proof that nurture is stronger than nature—that's one of the reasons I'm writing this book. Every conversation with Diane and every word that I'm writing here is another deposit on my ability to live my dream life.

Inflammation Is How the Body Heals Itself, but Chronic Inflammation Makes It Sick

Along with epigenetics, there's another connection between body and mind that can have a lasting impact: inflammation.

Inflammation is designed to be a healing response. When your body detects an intruder—thorn, bee sting, virus, or bacteria—it launches an inflammatory response to neutralize or remove the threat. This response is a cascade of multiple processes (think of your body calling in the army, navy, and air force), including increased flow of blood to the area of injury or infection and the dispatching of white blood cells to the region, which attempt to fight the invaders. You can quickly recognize the symptoms: pain, swelling, redness, and heat or fever. If the cascade is successful, the inflammation is acute—it dissipates in hours or days.

Chronic inflammation, on the other hand, can persist for months or years, even after the initial provocation is long

The quality of our lives is directly related to the quality of the stories we tell ourselves.

gone. The body can also mistakenly perceive its own cells or tissues as harmful, triggering an inflammatory response, even when there are no invaders that threaten its safety, which can result in an autoimmune disorder, such as rheumatoid arthritis or some thyroid disorders. Chronic inflammation can also result in disorders such as type 2 diabetes, cardiac disease, and obesity.

And your physical and mental health are inextricably linked. There is a mountain of evidence showing that physical inflammatory disorders, such as diabetes, obesity, or heart disease, increase the risk for developing a mental illness. Likewise, if you have a mental illness, you're at greater risk for developing a physical illness. And, according to the National Library of Medicine, both social isolation and loneliness are major risk factors for poor physical and mental health status, through enhanced chronic inflammation.

It might surprise you to know that chronic inflammation is associated with almost all mental illnesses, especially if they are chronic and severe, including depression. The hypothalamic-pituitary-adrenal axis (HPAA), which is the stress-response center of the brain, helps the body to rapidly and effectively respond to a threat. Chronic inflammation starts when the HPAA goes into constant overdrive as a result of chronic stress. HPAA overdrive can ultimately provoke some brain cells to produce pro-inflammatory cytokines—inflammatory proteins that can prevent other brain cells from working normally, resulting in even more inflammation.

Critically, the stress-induced inflammatory response can cause affected brain cells to reduce or stop producing brain-derived neurotropic factor (BDNF). Think of BDNF as an essential fertilizer, necessary for brain cells to grow, multiply, and form many strong connections with other brain cells. Without adequate BDNF, neurons, the brain cells that send electrical information around the brain and throughout the body, shrink and die.

When chronic inflammation causes neurons to shrink or die, it can be seen on brain images, such as an MRI, especially in the hippocampus—a small, curved part of the brain that is involved in the formation of new memories and is also associated with learning and emotions. When you look at the brains of people with severe or chronic depression, you can see they have reduced hippocampal volume.

Antidepressants work by provoking an increase in BDNF, which ultimately leads to the growth of new brain cells. Exercise performs the same function, as does eating a Mediterranean diet, engaging with a supportive community, and likely other activities that support our mental health, such as practicing one's faith or interacting with a beloved pet. Talk therapy, also known as psychotherapy, likely impacts BDNF as well, although this hasn't been clearly demonstrated in empirical research. However, several types of psychotherapy have been demonstrated to provide significant benefit for the treatment of depression, anxiety, and other psychiatric disorders.

Consciously trying to transform your thoughts, actions, and interactions can strengthen your anti-inflammatory arsenal. By achieving and celebrating small wins, you can bolster your sense of agency and have greater control of your emotions and moods. Personal power comes from consciously assigning positive meaning to your experiences, including your setbacks or mishaps. Diane says she is "constantly searching for the win, especially when it's not even remotely obvious." The quality of our lives is directly related to the quality of the stories we tell ourselves and other people. How we communicate with ourselves and others truly impacts our resilience, protecting us from mental and physical illness.

Culture is really the collection of stories that people consistently share with each other. You can't always control what happens to you, but you can always control the story you tell about your experience. Sitting in negativity blocks the path to solutions. If you assume a victim stance, you may become powerless, resentful, and angry. If you consistently seek someone or something to blame, looking for scapegoats rather than solutions, over time you will become less resilient, and thus more vulnerable. Just own it. Build your response-ability by taking responsibility and the solutions will follow.

THE QUICK WIN

Diane is a BDNF junkie. She often gives presentations to her physician colleagues about the inflammatory basis of depression and anxiety and the role BDNF plays in recovery. While her area of professional expertise is psychopharmacology (the safe, appropriate, personalized prescribing of psychiatric medications), she also believes in the power of psychotherapy and other complementary therapies, like exercise and a Mediterranean diet. "There is scientific evidence that supports the inclusion of many alternative modalities in holistic mental health care," Diane notes. "But you can't yoga your way out of a severe depression. However, yoga, other physical activities, mindfulness, and a diet that leans heavily on vegetables and healthy fats can be a critical protection against mental illness. For some of my patients, exercise is a drug. It didn't get them well, but it certainly helped, and I have no doubt exercise also helps to keep them well."

Think about all the ways you can boost your BDNF. Reflect on your own self-talk—do you bully yourself, or does your internal narrative empower you to win? Changing how you talk to yourself starts with awareness. If your internal narrative includes calling yourself a loser, constantly criticizing, and never lifting you up, it's time to confront those thoughts and stop them in their tracks. Sometimes that requires help from a therapist, but once you recognize you're bullying yourself, it's possible to catch yourself in the act and change your narrative. While it might seem difficult in the beginning, the more you do it, the more second nature it becomes.

10

Remake Your Memories to Enrich Your Future

DIANE SHARES this searing story told by one of her patients in her book *This Is Depression*:

> I was sexually abused by my stepfather. For years, I thought it was my fault. I still can't think about all the reasons I believed that was the case, but I knew I was to blame. When I told my mother, she chose him over me. That led to years of feeling dirty, unlovable, and worthless. I chose bad boyfriends and two bad husbands because I didn't think I deserved better. Then I got depressed. I know this will sound ridiculous, but getting depressed was both the best and the worst thing that ever happened to me. Don't get me wrong: it was

> horrible. I felt hopeless and I knew I would never recover. But once I found the right doctor and accepted that I needed treatment, I was finally able to face my past and how sexual and emotional abuse made me vulnerable to depression. Most importantly, I learned it wasn't my fault. It took me years to accept that I was a child, and he was 100 percent responsible, and once I did accept that, I was finally free. I still find it hard to trust people, and I am still working on myself, but I don't see myself as hopelessly broken anymore.

Out of terrible experiences, beautiful breakthroughs are born. This story resonated powerfully with me because it expressed the key themes of my life so far—abuse, self-loathing, perceived injustice, depression, treatment, recovery, vulnerability, reinvention, freedom, and possibility. You might be seeing aspects of your own life through this patient's lens right now. Her willingness to share is powerfully important because so many people with similar stories feel so alone, like they're the only one who has those experiences and is suffering their painful repercussions. Think about what you're willing to share and with whom you're willing to share it. By sharing our personal stories, we give other people permission to do the same. And by allowing them to share their stories, we liberate them from the powerful hold their stories may have on them. We call these kind of exchanges *cathartic conversations* because they open the space for people to redefine the impact of their past on their future.

We are the sum of all our memories. Every experience shapes our psyche through the emotions that we associate with it. People assume that the real drivers of their decisions are rational, but the real drivers are "e-rational." E-rational isn't irrational. It's the fusion of emotion and rational. It's the collection of feelings, relationships, perceptions, values, deep beliefs, and biochemistry that make up who we are.

There is no such thing as an exact memory. Our memories are constantly changing. Every time we recall them, we open them up to new interpretation. New influences and discoveries impact the way we review our past. We can unconsciously alter our memories, but we can also consciously apply empowering meaning to whatever we've been through.

Remember the hippocampus from last chapter? It's the part of our brain that assigns meaning to experiences. The more intense the meaning, the more significant the memory. By recalibrating our recollection of our experiences, we can reassign different emotions to them. We can turn whatever happened, however traumatic, into sources of strength. We can interpret what has happened as a way of expanding our belief in ourselves.

So, when I think about my recovery from clinical depression or when Diane thinks about her comeback from burnout, we consistently make deposits in our personal confidence accounts. We focus on achieving the empowering result, not reliving the original trauma.

"Wow, I Never Thought of It That Way Before"

The problem with memories is that they visit you at the most inopportune moments. We've all seen people stopped by something that only they can see or feel. When we prompt them with a gentle question like, "Are you OK?" or "What just happened there?" or "Where did you go?" they shake their heads and either share their momentary hiatus or simply say "Nothing" and struggle to get back into the conversation. As a Keeper of the Safety Flame, you can follow up with someone in private after the moment has passed and also prompt others to share their ghosts with you. You'll be amazed at how willing people are to talk about their innermost fears if they trust you. In fact, you can measure your trust by the secrets others share with you.

If we don't take charge of our memories, they can constrain and even cripple us. Every one of the clients I coach is wrestling with bogeymen from their past. That's why they're talking to me in the first place. The best phrase I can ever hear from them is, "Wow, I never thought of it that way before." By reframing their past, they recreate their future. It requires a heightened level of self-awareness, but like any muscle, it gets stronger with vigorous use.

As a valued mentor once told me, the problem with life is that it is so daily. On any given day, you may have multiple interactions with multiple people. Most will be within the realm of normal—they will go more or less the way you expect them to go. A few will be spectacular—they will thrill, surprise, and delight you. And a few will be horrible—they will shock, dismay, and unnerve you. The bad experiences could be due to something the other person did or because of something stupid that you did. The danger is allowing the bad experience to dominate your mind. Instead, reflect on how you could have handled the situation better. Apologize if you need to. Forgive if you need to. But don't let the memory derail you.

This is deep work. It's difficult work. But it's work that must be done. Self-reflection is the path to self-mastery. And self-mastery is the prelude to helping others master themselves. Until you can free yourself of misguided guilt or unresolved anger or inner impotence, you cannot create a place where others feel like they belong. You will be held back by your own ghosts and demons.

THE QUICK WIN

Diane has treated many patients with post-traumatic stress disorder (PTSD) and learned some of her most enduring life lessons from them. She shared, "Firstly, trauma is subjective—what is traumatic to me might not be traumatic to you. Secondly, trauma is cumulative—I can never recall diagnosing PTSD in someone who didn't have multiple traumatic events, often starting with childhood abuse, neglect, or chaos. Sometimes, what seems like an innocuous event, like a minor car accident, becomes the straw that breaks the camel's back.

"This makes the diagnosis challenging, so I learned to look at my patient's entire life experience, not just the traumatic event. Finally, out of the most horrible experiences, good things can come. For me, this was a life-changing revelation. To have several patients who had experienced something so terrifying or horrifying and who were recovering from PTSD say, 'I would never have asked for that to happen, but in some ways I'm glad it did because this incredibly good thing wouldn't have happened,' blew me away. Oddly, that revelation brought me a sense of safety—and led me to believe there is always a path ahead."

Think about whether you're comfortable having cathartic conversations, whether it's your opening up to people you trust or being a person who is able to hold someone's emotions when they share them, without absorbing them yourself. If you're not comfortable sharing or receiving emotional content, explore the reasons why. This can help you understand some barrier you might be experiencing in your relationships with others. If you feel you're already

successfully navigating emotional discussions, think about how you can share your expertise with others who might be less comfortable or completely avoidant. Share the value of remaking their memories or reframing their experiences.

11

Redefine Your Relationship to Risk

THE COVID PANDEMIC has caused many of us, perhaps for the first time, to evaluate our sense of safety in our day-to-day lives and reconsider our relationship with risk.

As the pandemic progressed, it ultimately gave rise to what Diane refers to as the COVID mental illness trifecta—health anxiety, financial stress, and the impact of prolonged isolation and loneliness—resulting in a worldwide increase in mental illness, especially depression and anxiety, even among people who were not previously considered vulnerable. This is likely due to the chronic and unpredictable nature of pandemic-related stress. Stress that is chronic and unpredictable is also the most debilitating—it is known to cause changes in the structure and function of the brain and can result in depression, anxiety, and dementia. The chronic, unpredictable pandemic-related stress continuously assaulted our senses, hijacking our brain through emotional shocks that were random, severe, and defied preparation because they were also unprecedented.

Life is all about ups and downs. In fact, you can't really appreciate the joys of life without having some experience with the contrasting emotions of hurt, sadness, and fear. Every day, billions of attempted "micro-hijackings" of the brain occur as the amygdala reacts to real or perceived threats. The amygdala is a structure nestled in the middle of the brain that regulates emotional responses to environmental threats and challenges. It also ties meaning to memories and is involved in reward processing and decision-making.

When it's operating optimally, the amygdala enables us to successfully navigate the ups and downs of everyday life. But when it's overwhelmed with stress, especially the chronic, unpredictable kind, the amygdala can flood us with fear and provoke panic. Importantly, the amygdala is highly influenced by our interpretation of an event—the event itself is less important than how the event makes us feel. For instance, a get-together with new colleagues might not seem like a big deal, and certainly not something that should provoke terror. However, if you have social anxiety disorder, your amygdala might interpret the casual get-together as terrifying, leading you to endure the event with significant discomfort and escape as soon as possible, or avoid it entirely.

Create Your Inner Shield

One defensive weapon in the battle against chronic, unpredictable stress is the creation (or reinforcement) of your inner shield. This critical emotional shield supports the existential certainty that you will survive, and even thrive, in any life

In the absence of effective parenting, you can parent yourself.

situation. Your inner shield helps to maintain your conviction that you're OK—or that you'll be OK—by deflecting the negative forces around you. Instead of absorbing negativity and allowing it to impact your own thoughts, feelings, and behaviours, a robust inner shield reinforces your resilience or coping skills and sustains your belief in yourself. It's your protection against panic, desperation, or despair.

Your inner shield isn't a static entity. It's like a personal force field, constantly adapting in response to your external environment. You'll still feel fear and doubt and even short bursts of anxiety, but you'll always feel empowered to succeed because you rule the one person who controls how you think, feel, and behave: yourself.

For most people, their inner shield started developing in childhood, fortified by loving, supportive parents, grandparents, teachers, friends, and anyone else who, through their words and deeds, built them up and helped them to be their best self. Those who've had a difficult childhood, facing chaos, neglect, or abuse, might not develop a strong inner shield, making them more vulnerable to the negative forces that are part of adult life. An inadequate inner shield can lead you to absorb the anger, distress, or frustration of others. Ultimately, taking on someone else's problems, or feeling personally diminished by another person's bad behaviour, has an impact on our own mental health.

The good news is, regardless of your childhood experience, it is possible to build or strengthen your inner shield. Additionally, as we mature, our inner shield increasingly interlocks with the inner shields of the people around us—our children, other loved ones, co-workers, and friends. By supporting and strengthening others' inner shield, we reinforce our own. This is one aspect of building resilience.

In the absence of effective parenting, you can parent yourself. After a lifetime of panic attacks, depression, professional failures, and financial setbacks, I've learned to step back and counsel myself. When I'm behaving like Adolescent Mike, or Maladaptive Mike, I remind myself that I'm now Wise Mike, Elder Mike, or Mentor Mike. Once I've done that, I can provide the less mature Mike with the compassion and perspective that I didn't get growing up. I'm acutely conscious of my inner dialogue. I'm on a permanent mental diet that feeds my sense of safety. I don't lambaste myself for being stupid anymore. Rather, I observe that I behaved stupidly. I learned my lesson, and I resolve never to behave that way again. It's my action, not myself, that needs to be sanctioned.

THE QUICK WIN

Catch yourself passing judgement on yourself. Strengthen your inner shield by identifying the behaviour or the way of thinking that you resolve to change. Then celebrate yourself when you actually do it.

1. **Believe in Your Ability to Surmount Any Difficulty**
2. **Accept That You Might Need to Endure Temporary Confusion or Uncertainty**
3. **Commit to Finding New Mental Models to Master the New Realities**
4. **Find People to Support You through Crises**
5. **Build Your Strategy and Then Take Action**

5 WAYS TO CREATE YOUR OWN PREDICTABILITY

NO ONE IS NATURALLY FEARLESS. They may just appear that way because of their willingness to take on their fears and act boldly. They've created their own predictability through consciously adopting the five learned behaviours:

1. Believe in Your Ability to Surmount Any Difficulty

Look back at your triumphs and recoveries. Acknowledge your personal strengths. Remind yourself of your resourcefulness. Trust yourself to come back stronger and smarter from any challenge you encounter. Expect to be a victor not a victim. By picking up your own shield, you create your own safe space that nothing can penetrate.

2. Accept That You Might Need to Endure Temporary Confusion or Uncertainty

The beginning of any struggle is often characterized by ambiguity and vagueness. It's like a heavy fog—it will always dissipate. Any challenge must be faced with urgency and patience in equal measure. Patience is not the same as inaction. It's preparing to act when the time is right. Mastering the tension between urgency and patience is a matter of experience.

An important aspect of being mindful is accepting that facing a crisis is a part of life. Diane says, "I've learned that you must allow your worries in the front door and show them out the back door, but don't serve them tea." That means that we all have worries and fears and it's important to acknowledge them (let them in the front door). Failing to do so keeps them repressed and they bleed into our thoughts, feelings, and behaviours, often in negative ways. Showing your worries out the back door without serving tea means we should acknowledge them but we can't ruminate on them and allow them to take over. Face them, accept them, learn from them, and move forward. Diane adds, "I have to say to myself, 'Yup, that's a problem,' and then I shift my focus, as quickly as possible, to finding a solution."

Discern the difference between risk and recklessness. There is prudent risk and irresponsible risk. The first requires planning, practice, and forethought. The second entails arrogance, laziness, or disregard for the consequences of one's actions. For example, most people don't know the basics of heart health—blood pressure, body mass index (BMI), or cholesterol levels. The data is out there but they don't study it. So they live a life that increases their odds of early mortality instead of decreasing them. Planning mitigates risk. Impulsivity increases it.

Diane speaks about maturity in terms of brain development. "The prefrontal cortex (PFC) sits at the front of the brain, right behind the forehead. Its location seems perfect to me because its job is to be the brain's CEO. The PFC is responsible for executive functioning—organizing, planning, critical thinking, and forward thinking (thinking ahead)." It won't surprise readers to learn that the PFC is also one of the last brain regions to fully mature—on average, by age twenty-five. Of course, some PFCs mature much earlier while others might never have great executive functioning.

Diane adds, “Children rely on their parents, teachers, and coaches to help them to make good choices. Essentially, we are our children’s PFCs until theirs is working optimally. This also explains why we need to tell children the same thing over and over and over again. They learn quickly because their neurons are constantly wiring and rewiring, but the choices they make, despite our belief that they should know better, often lack critical thinking or consideration of potential negative outcomes.”

A lack of thoughtful consideration isn’t just the purview of youth. Adults also tend to underappreciate future risk, even if presented with expert guidance. We also forget lessons from the past, especially if the experience was negative. Finally, if we’re unsure of next steps, too often we rely on guidance from people who are just as likely to misjudge a situation and make the same mistakes. The life-threatening fires and storms the world is now facing with increasing frequency would be far less deadly if we were able to break through our dysfunctional mental models and appropriately prepare for potential disasters. Yet, despite mountains of science and the accessibility of expert advice, people continue to ignore evacuation orders, build with unsafe materials, or refuse to take other steps to mitigate risk.

Working with a person who is reckless—taking unnecessary, irresponsible risks—can rapidly obliterate team safety and might even destroy a business. Whether due to inexperience, immaturity, or hubris, recklessness can cause irreparable harm. The title of *You Belong Here* includes the subtitle *How to Make People Feel Safe to Be Their Best, Take Bold Risks, and Win*. Taking bold risks must include reliance on a mature PFC.

3. Commit to Finding New Mental Models to Master the New Realities

What worked yesterday may not work tomorrow. Letting go of your mental models when they become invalid is central to creating your own predictability. A mental model is how you make sense of the world. It is also a set of shared beliefs that comes from our experiences, the influences of others, and our personal identity. Mental models are maintained by conscious and unconscious signals that drive our behaviours.

As the world changes, your mental models need to change. This requires an awareness of the need to change. The signals are clear: you're not achieving your desired results; others are moving away from you not toward you; you're unhappy; anxiety is your default emotion. The problem is that mental models are not built to change, which is why it's so difficult to change a system.

Examples of constraining mental models are:

- "I'm a doctor, and I don't believe that my patients can understand or cope with medical information so I decide what to share with them, and I don't share what I know they can't handle."
- "I'm just a salesperson. I don't get asked about strategy, so I'm not responsible for it. The only way to sell is to pressure customers into buying and extract as much money as I can."
- "They're telling us to evacuate because of the hurricane, but it's never as bad as they say it will be."
- "I'm not paid to be creative or imaginative. I just do what I'm told."
- "I know it doesn't make sense, but this is how it's always been done."

On the other hand, examples of liberating mental models are:

- "As a doctor, I am a navigator, and patients are captains of their own health care journey. My role is an informed guide and educator, to ensure my patients are able to make informed health care decisions."
- "The best way to sell is to understand my customer's strategy for success and align with it. Making customers want to buy is much better than trying to pressure them into buying."
- "Throughout my life, I have proven that I am creative and resourceful. I can control what I do and how I do it. I'm becoming better all the time."
- "A flexible, agile culture will always beat a bureaucratic one. Discipline and structure can be empowering as long as they are responsive to dynamic change."
- "Our job is to earn an attractive income by enriching our customers' lives."

No matter how long you've believed in your mental model or invested in it, you need to jettison it when it's proven to be obsolete. Be candid with yourself when that moment comes. It's always hard, but trying to manage the world through an obsolete mental model will crush you and, potentially, your teammates. We've all witnessed what happens to people who refuse to change. They attempt to justify unsustainable positions. They lose their touch and get left behind or let go. Then they get bitter, not better.

Critically, a crisis is an opportunity to break free from a tired and ineffective mental model. Failing to respond to a crisis with new approaches that create positive, enduring change will lead to a return of the status quo. If that happens repeatedly, people will lose hope and become disengaged.

4. Find People to Support You through Crises

Your greatest security may be the calibre of people who stand ready to create the future with you. Explore how they can help you but also how you can help them. Become the person that attracts the very best people. Go looking for them now. Don't wait until you're in a crisis before you look for a resource.

This book is a big step in the right direction. Diane and I are now part of your interlocking inner shield. We stand with you in your quest for personal safety and inner certainty. By reading these words, you are reciprocating our support. You are validating our raison d'être—to change the world, one person at a time. By co-creating our interlocking shield together, we are vanquishing the real enemy: isolation—the feeling of being alone, disconnected, and in peril. We're moving forward as a collective whole. We're grateful for the privilege.

5. Build Your Strategy and Then Take Action

Create your own personal rituals and best practices that bring you predictable results and most consistently deliver your desired outcomes. Be agile—continually monitor your impact and effectiveness so you can pivot where necessary. Get help when you need it.

Reflect on your experiences but don't ruminate. Ruminate means to churn a thought repeatedly through your mind without learning from it. Think about your experiences as a platform to improve, not as punishment for what you did. Repeating your effective actions yields success.

Repeating your failures, even if it's just constantly reliving your mistakes, will ruin you.

One of my strategies that has proven highly effective is to live every day as though my life depends on it—because it does. Each day is the only day I can control. If I make my day great, it sets me up for success the next day. If I don't, I have to recover my momentum the next day. I will do anything to pre-empt even one bad day if the means of pre-emption are within my control. For example, preparing thoroughly for a presentation or key conversation, or doing something now rather than procrastinating so I don't suffer regret, or avoiding over-consumption that will lead to a next-day hangover, or following a ritual that thrusts me into the right mindset for a challenging task.

Instead of a post-mortem, I like to do a pre-mortem that obviates avoidable mistakes. It's called prospective hindsight—imagining that an event has already occurred. According to research by Deborah Mitchell, Jay Russo, and Nancy Pennington, prospective hindsight can increase the ability to correctly identify reasons for future outcomes by 30 percent. It's one of the ways I create my own predictability. Instead of rewiring my brain based on past missteps, I prewire my brain for future breakthroughs. This entire book is written with a pre-mortem mindset: What will readers find most useful and inspirational? What will motivate the maximum number of people to pass on a positive recommendation about this book? What will enable Diane and me to have the greatest impact on people's sense of safety and willingness to take prudent risks?

I

Creating Belonging in a Hybrid World

III

Owning Your Power

II

Growing Enriching Relationships

Winning on the Brink

V

Showing the Way

PART IV

WINNING ON THE BRINK

12

Understand That Pressure Is the Price You Pay for Success

I'M WRITING THESE WORDS at 4:10 p.m. on Sunday, March 19, 2023. I've promised Diane and my publisher, Page Two, that the first draft of the manuscript will be completed by the end of April 2023—just six weeks away. Between now and then, I also have major consulting and speaking commitments that are huge time sucks. I absolutely, positively have to finish the manuscript in order to make the 2024 Spring launch calendar. The pressure is on. I'm also in a state of mild panic. I've made commitments that I don't know how I can honour—but I know I will. Together with Diane, I'll find a way.

I know you empathize with me. If you're up to big things, you're probably in the same boat as me. You're taking on ambitious tasks with talented people who are holding you to the highest standards. You're feeling the heat. There are days when you regret taking on the challenge. The spectre of failure haunts you. You can already feel the humiliation of making excuses to people whom you've disappointed. But then you realize there is no other way. This is who you are. You are someone who needs to create, produce, contribute, build, inspire, and lead.

The decision to pay the price frees you to pursue the possibility. It liberates you from your alibis. You give up the right to give up. You find another gear. You discover deeper resources. You reach out to more people. You ignite your imagination and creativity.

It takes a special kind of crazy to enthusiastically embrace pressure and panic. It's the kind of crazy that believes you can defy the odds, define the future, live the dream. You can blaze a trail for others to follow.

That's the kind of crazy that makes other people feel safe. They depend on you to create new possibilities for them to make good on. They're willing to do the work because you've shown them the path forward—in ways both big and small. You've demonstrated that it can be done, and they can do it.

Feel Scared and Safe at the Same Time

Can you think of a moment when you felt scared and safe at the same time? Maybe it was when you were watching a horror movie. You felt scared for the characters on the screen while you munched your popcorn or sipped your soda. Or maybe it was on a rollercoaster ride, where you felt the fear but knew you would be just fine at the end of the ride. Or maybe it was skydiving, moving to a new country, joining a new company, going on a first date, or even getting married. In every case, you felt the good fear that precedes a desired outcome.

Some fear is normal. It rouses the amygdala to process your sensory information and deliver the fight or flight response so you can protect yourself. Your heart rate rises. Your vision becomes more acute. You access your inner superpowers. And less essential parts of your body slow down so you can maximize your available resources.

Anxiety is fear gone bad. You feel like you've lost control of yourself. Everything becomes a threat. You're enveloped in a sense of dread and doom. Your functioning is impaired even when you're in a completely safe space. You feel shaky and weak. You become your own adversary.

Pay attention to the source of your fears. Is it internal or external? It is it real or imagined? Does it originate from a mental model that should be replaced by a newer one or is it an outworn habit that should be discarded for good? Unless you're in a genuinely threatening situation like a war zone, a dark alley, or an actual fist fight, you could be conjuring up your own dark thoughts. In a hurricane, get to the basement. In a snowstorm, stay home. But sitting at your desk on a sunny day, it must be possible to conjure up thoughts that energize and empower you. If you're being controlled by anxiety, it is absolutely possible to take back control of your thoughts, feelings, and behaviours.

That's why a coach, confidante, advisor, partner, or mentor is so valuable. They provide us with a view of what we can do and who we can become. They offer a set of insights that can help us grow. They're another level of support in our personal growth infrastructure. That said, if your fear or anxiety is intractable, persistent, and impacting your ability to function, it's time to call in some reinforcements—a family doctor can assess you and determine what kind of support might be most helpful.

No matter how prepared, prudent, or conscientious you are, some deniability of danger is required to create your own predictability. You need to calibrate your anxiety sensitivities. Fear what's appropriate to the situation. There is a fine line between living life to the full and jeopardizing your well-being. When we drive, we fasten our seatbelt and take out insurance but never expect to be involved in a serious car accident. When we walk through the urban core, we deny the possibility of being assaulted or mugged. When we work with colleagues, we never expect them to become abusive or violent.

Educated deniability is integral to feeling safe. Of course, random accidents and incidents can happen, and we need to be vigilant against them. Most situations we encounter are not inherently risky. Assigning risk to innocuous situations is a sign of chronic anxiety—the never-ending "what if..." that is characteristic thinking associated with generalized anxiety disorder. Everything, even everyday events, becomes a potential threat. Chronically anxious people are not capable of engaging in continual, reasoned risk assessment, because every situation is assigned an elevated level of risk.

Let's go back to the good fear. In its simplest form, it's the fear that makes you do things you'd probably prefer to avoid: studying for an exam, keeping on top of the housework, or visiting your great aunt whose house smells of mothballs. The fear of failing, having to spend an entire weekend shovelling out your place, or upsetting your parents ignites a desire to do those distasteful things. But good fear is also the nervousness that animates and excites you. It's when you take on an ambitious endeavour or make a big promise that will test and stretch you. It's the thing that draws you out of your comfort zone, compelling you to face failure so you can tap into your reservoir of power. Good fear is what you feel when you're more afraid of *not* doing it.

I recently coached a woman called Karen who is a newly minted partner at a major consulting firm. She was invited to deliver a keynote to a thousand other partners at her firm's annual conference. Public speaking is not a normal part of her daily responsibilities, so she didn't regard herself as a skilled orator. She was so nervous she felt nauseous. Then I asked her: "How would you feel if you were told you didn't need to speak because they had found someone better?" She paused for a moment before saying, "Terrible." After that, she leaned into her task. She still felt tense, but her entire attitude changed. The challenge of preparing for the role was nowhere near as scary as not even being considered for the role. She crushed it.

Don't Beat Yourself Up, Build Yourself Up

Pressure is crucial for building resilience—the ability to adapt or recover from change, or to withstand difficulty. Every moment life changes. Our bodies change. Our minds change. We age. We can never go back to the way things were, only forward to the way they're going to be. Understanding that fact is the essence of success and happiness. Instead of thinking about what's lost, we need to think about the opportunities ahead.

This is an advanced thinking process that isn't possible when we're depressed and can't think outside the black box. But when we're healthy, we can train our brain to look forward to opportunity. Most importantly, we can permit ourselves the pain of messing up, knowing that it can be alchemized into power if we process it the right way. That's why we need other people. We can't see things clearly without their perspective. Ultimately, it's our choice, but the best choice is an informed one.

A win is when the right person gets the right opportunity at the right time. That's a whole load of "right" all at once, but, as Diane says, "What's for you won't go past you." A missed opportunity, a pitch that didn't make the cut, or the role you didn't win are all tough pills to swallow. But, if you take the time to understand why it wasn't your win, you'll be more likely to win the next time. If you sink into misery and decide that you're hopeless, you'll be more likely to lose the next opportunity. Sometimes you're the right person but you're too busy, so it's the wrong time. If it's for you, it won't go past you, so long as you're ready to win. You get ready by preparing and part of preparing is learning from your mistakes.

Everyone has feelings of regret or disappointment. That's normal. But dwelling on them for too long can cause undue anxiety. Let the upset in the front door and let it out the back door but don't serve it tea. When you lose an opportunity, just know a new opportunity will come along. Compassionately reflect on your actions. Own the outcome. Don't blame others for causing your upset. The more you practice thinking this way, the more you wire your brain into automatically doing so.

There are many ways to find calm: taking deep breaths, chanting a mantra, thinking of something you have to look forward to, visualizing your loved ones, being physically active, hugging your pets, getting outside and being with trees, eating the right foods, listening to your favourite music, talking to a trusted confidante, doing something for somebody. Find your own way to calm and center yourself in the face of challenge and change, and call it what you want: mindfulness, meditation, reflection, prayer, taking a break. We all have an enormous capacity to control ourselves in ways that we may not always realize. It begins with accepting the situation as reality. Then you need to reflect on what it really means to you. Then you need to deliberately make peace with it.

A key motif that I've referenced throughout this book is to monitor your inner dialogue. Listen to how you talk to yourself and how you talk to others. Ask yourself if you're nurturing yourself and others or negating them. The way you speak about your reality becomes your reality. We live inside our words. Rather than beating yourself up, which worsens the situation, speaking empathically to yourself allows you to move forward. Rather than "You loser," tell yourself, "You did the best you could under the circumstances" or "You'll learn from this and do better next time." Our speech inspires others to raise their game, or it infects them to constrain it.

Don't use phrases like "I'm rambling" or "I don't know if I'm making sense." They discount the value of what you've just said. Resist the temptation to minimize yourself. Leave people with the belief in the power of what you've just said. Being overly modest can also come across as false or disingenuous.

And then, when you are standing firm on your own foundation, you can lift others up, help them belong, create safety for them. Don't diminish others—don't call them names or gripe about them. Diminishing others diminishes you more. Talking ugly makes you ugly. Have you noticed how hard it is to be with someone who constantly diminishes others? Just being near them brings you down. Be the person who raises everyone up.

Falling down is the price for staying upright.

Failure Is a Sign That You're Winning

The more pressure you can handle, the greater the difficulties and change you'll be able to master. There are a certain number of rejections, failures, and setbacks that are the rhythm of life. They are grist for the mill. They need to be built into your process and measured accordingly. They are proof that everything is going the way it should. They build the required muscle to overcome resistance. Their absence signifies a problem.

In the world of investing, a pattern of returns that does not reflect variability could indicate fraud. In the world of baseball, the average Hall of Famer hit .303 with on-base percentage of .376—that means in over six out of ten times they got up to bat, they did neither. When babies are learning to walk, they fall on average seventeen times an hour. Given that frequency of falls, you might think their little brains carefully computed all that negative input so they could learn from their errors. Apparently, that's just not so. Their innate drive to ambulate understands that falling down is the price for staying upright.

Failure is a sign that you're winning. Winners will always lose more than losers because they're trying more things. Their hunger for success is greater than their fear of falling short. The more ambitious your goals, the more resistance you should expect. The blockbuster *Chicken Soup for the Soul* self-help book was rejected 144 times by publishers before it became a bestseller, and then a series, and now a multi-armed franchise. "If we had given up after one hundred publishers, I likely would not be where I am now," Jack Canfield, the author, wrote. "I encourage you to reject rejection. If someone says no, just say NEXT!"

Just like a Hall of Famer, you need to know what your win-loss ratio is telling you. In some areas of your life, you may be confronted with a series of losses before you win—like Jack Canfield. In other areas of life, you need to achieve the win that sustains your belief in yourself. Just like setbacks are inevitable, wins are vital. They are proof of your potency. So set yourself up for success by recognizing and celebrating every win—no matter how small. We can lose our self-confidence if we don't constantly replenish it. This is especially important for newcomers or rookies who may not have a record of success yet. They need to believe in their desired future state.

As we mature into our chosen professions, we need to understand the standards of performance excellence (SOPE) that measure our levels of achievement relative to our peers and competitors. SOPE range from customer reviews to closing rates to cost efficiencies to acquisition and retention of accounts—anything that indicates your performance against valid benchmarks. SOPE are sources of constructive pressure that challenge you to surpass the prevailing standards. If you don't know your SOPE, you cannot confirm your true status as a frontrunner or potential GOAT.

My SOPE are:

- Partnering with key opinion leaders like Diane to create new content like *You Belong Here*.
- Being rated highly by key stakeholders such as clients and industry commentators.
- Sustaining the loyalty and followership of long-standing supporters.
- Earning a seat at the C-suite table so I can make a difference with them.
- Achieving my commercial goals as an entrepreneur.

- Maximizing my contribution of time and money to pro bono and community-building activities.
- Winning opportunities to partner with marquee organizations on how to help their people create a sense of belonging.
- Ensuring that people who have placed their trust in me feel like it was the best thing they could have done.

The opposite of SOPE is DOPE: delusions of peoples' experiences. DOPE comes from feeling less than others because of what their social media say about their lifestyles. We should be aware that social media lives are fictitious—their images reflect the fiction that they want others to believe. The mistake is to believe that they are real and judge oneself against them. From now on, consume others' social media as the reality shows they really are.

THE QUICK WIN

Diane detests social media, having learned early on that the content too often reflects a false, unattainable perfection. "No one shares their problem with hemorrhoids on their social media profile," she says. And the pile-on effect resulting from a misguided post or poorly considered message can be devastating, especially for younger people. "I made a decision early on in my social media journey—I don't read nasty responses, because I'm not interested in negativity. That also means I never send impulsive posts, which are more likely to be ill-considered. Because a social media presence is important for my work, I have teammates who can provide a sober second thought before anything goes out and ensure my message is consistent and thoughtful. If I want to communicate about what's happening in my personal life, I find a phone call, text message, or get-together much more meaningful and safer."

Think about the tools you currently employ to weather a crisis and calm your mind. If you don't have a method, explore options, such as a mindfulness app. Identify your top five standards of personal excellence (SOPE) and live them.

13

Accept That Living on the Brink Is the Cost of Creating Breakthroughs

ON A RECENT TRIP to Encinitas, a small coastal city in Southern California, I went for a walk along the cliffs just above the beach. The very edge of the cliffs are gradually crumbling. There are signs that say, "WARNING: BLUFF AND TRAIL UNSTABLE. USE AT YOUR OWN RISK." Rather than being obvious, the signs felt oddly profound, given what we've all just lived through. Many of us fear that at any moment our world can crumble and crash into the sea. COVID exacerbated that fear of collapse. The unimaginable seemed entirely possible, even probable.

The word "brink" refers to the extreme edge of land before a steep or vertical slope. It's also defined as the verge or the threshold of danger. Some of the most valuable real estate in the world is perched on edges of land before a steep slope into the ocean. It's incredibly difficult to build on the brink, but the brave (and rich) are rewarded with unobstructed, incomparable views. The most significant accomplishments are achieved at the very limits of endurance, making victory somehow sweeter. The most powerful inventions push the boundaries of what stood before. There is no such thing as coasting through a revolution—it takes all you have and then some. You must live, endure, and prosper on the brink before change is realized. Crisis is an opportunity—sometimes it's the most critical element in the process of provoking essential, meaningful, enduring change.

Both Diane and I are way too familiar with burnout—a work-related syndrome that occurs in occupations where others' needs come first, and where there are high demands, few resources, and a disconnect between a worker's expectations and their experiences. Burnout results in a state of emotional exhaustion, a declining sense of accomplishment, and a growing cynicism toward others.

Sometimes, we make ourselves more vulnerable to burnout. We push ourselves too hard and we take on too much until we can't go any further. We reach a level of exhaustion or distress where we're forced to pause and reconsider. Sound familiar? If you're up to something big in your life, you're going to take yourself to the brink, time and time again. As T.S. Eliot wrote, "Only those who will risk going too far can possibly find out how far one can go." The operative phrase is *risk going too far*, not *going too far*. Going too far, too often, can make it impossible to accomplish your goals.

Even highly adaptive people can struggle with burnout. I am coaching a gifted person called Phil, the founder and leader of a highly lucrative start-up. He's super smart, resourceful, and charming. He's also the consummate team player—generous and collaborative. Phil is so hungry for success that he tries to pursue every opportunity he sees. He knows when he is approaching the outer limits of his personal capacity, but he feels powerless to stop himself. He says it's like watching a car crash happen in slow motion. He simply can't allow himself to intentionally step back from the chase. My role is to help him make peace with his obsessive drive and scale his operation so others can hunt on his behalf.

When I told Diane about my work with Phil, she immediately identified with him. "I've always wanted to be a part of everything, at the expense of prioritizing what's really important to me. I can end up being everywhere and nowhere. Often that comes from not being able to say no. I've had to discipline myself to make decisions about my work based on my own priorities and values and let go of everything else. That was, and continues to be, very hard work."

The Road Back from Burnout

Even though Diane is a highly skilled and accomplished psychiatrist, she has struggled with burnout. None of us is immune. While burnout is often blamed on the sufferer, and Diane certainly accepts responsibility for how her actions didn't protect her from becoming burned out, it's critical to remember that the system or workplace we're in is often just as responsible, if not more so. For Diane, working in a medical system, undergoing bitter, painful experiences, where she felt her patients' needs were not a priority, or even that they would be safe, provoked a moral injury. Fighting a lonely battle to get her patients the safest, most tolerable treatments, to hold decision makers accountable, and to insist on following science and not the dollar, all contributed to her burnout. Being "everywhere," and struggling to say no, did not help.

Diane's burnout came as a shock, she says. "You could never have told me that I would become burned out because I loved caring for my patients. It was so important to me and I never seemed to tire of it. It was engaging, interesting, and, perhaps most importantly, I was helping people. The thing that tipped me over the edge was my belief in fairness and justice—not just conceptually but practically. But imminent justice is not real. Sometimes bad things happen to good people. Sometimes you can't fight city hall. I was frustrated with political decisions that blocked my patients' access to the right treatments and the lack of compassion they experienced when they were dealing with other providers. I felt responsible for my patients, and, naively, I also felt responsible for my profession and the behaviour of my colleagues. I wrote op-eds. I stood up for my patients. And then, sometimes even my patients told me that I wasn't doing enough for them."

As a clinician suffering from burnout, Diane is definitely not alone. The Canadian Medical Association, Canada's largest physician advocacy group, surveyed members in 2017 and learned that 31 percent reported a high degree of burnout. By November 2021, that number had risen to 53 percent. Diane said she wasn't surprised, but "really frightened" by those numbers, because of their implications for the health care system. "The fact that more than half of my colleagues are struggling with emotional exhaustion, hopelessness, and a loss of compassion is a disastrous harbinger of what is to come—more medical errors, greater harm to patients, less satisfaction with the care experience, and even greater barriers to access care, as doctors, nurses, pharmacists, and other health care professionals simply walk away from their profession."

Safe means always having people who will strengthen you when you're not strong.

To recover from burnout, Diane had to identify patterns. She always took on too much. She took her responsibilities seriously and she never wanted to disappoint anyone, including her patients, colleagues, or the companies she worked with. She had serious FOMO—new opportunities to learn, share, and grow felt impossible to decline. Critically, she found herself prioritizing everyone except those who meant the most to her: her family.

The road back from burnout required Diane to change her behaviour and her work. She took time away from patient care to write a book. She developed an educational program, PsychedUp, to amplify the educational support of her colleagues, providing high quality psychiatric education to mental health professionals. She took on a leadership role at Telus, a large Canadian telecommunication company. She shared, "Medicine moves at a glacial pace, but telcos move at lightning speed. Darren Entwistle, Telus' CEO, seemed to understand. He encouraged my desire to create meaningful change in mental health care delivery, which wasn't something I was used to in the medical world."

Despite the changes she's made, Diane says she's never fully recovered from burnout. That's because breaking out of a burnout cycle is difficult. First, you must have insight: nothing happens until you recognize you're burned out and something must change. Next, you need to make a plan to change because finding a path out of burnout takes reflection, preparation, and patience. Even more importantly, changing how you think, feel, and behave takes a great deal of time and effort. If you don't change these, you're bound to repeat the cycle. Third, addressing burnout requires system adjustments because at its core, it's a workplace challenge, not just a one-time problem to be solved. That aspect of recovery is often beyond our control.

We Need Others' Perspective and Caring

In her book *This Is Depression*, Diane writes about the value of the gifts we give ourselves. "They're the greatest gifts of all," she shares, adding, "One of the greatest gifts I've given myself is the complete belief that the only person on earth I can control is me. We can't control the thoughts, feelings, or behaviours of our partners, children, other family members, friends, or co-workers. Believing this, at a cellular level, takes time and work, but once you've done it, it will be freeing. Once you understand and accept that you can only control you, you'll stop trying to change or control anyone else. You'll use your energy to control what you can: your own thoughts, feelings, and behaviours."

As anyone struggling with a mental illness can tell you, not being able to control how you think, feel, and behave, especially as an adult (it's like being a kid with an immature brain), is highly distressing. When struggling with severe anxiety, with a hijacked amygdala controlling what we think ("I sound like an idiot") and how we feel ("I'm so uncomfortable") and behave ("I'm leaving"), most people feel out of control and don't know how to regain their sense of equanimity. Sometimes, anxiety can become chronic and start to impact one's ability to function at home, at work, and in social situations. That's when professional help should be considered. The good news is there are tools that can help to take back control or give you a sense of control for the first time.

Sometimes, we need someone to guide us out of our misery and help us to make and sustain a much-needed change. We need their perspective and caring. We need them to ask us the questions, provide us with suggestions, or simply direct us toward a corrective course of action. Ordinary molehills can mushroom into mountains without the intervention of trusted advisors. Sometimes, this role is best filled by a professional—a psychologist or clinical counsellor with expertise in the area of cognitive behavioural therapy (CBT). CBT has the most research evidence demonstrating its value in identifying, controlling, and changing dysfunctional thoughts and behaviours. However, we all have the ability to support and coach people in our network. This book will help you play this vital function.

Social Support Is Critical

Social support can take many forms—a loved one, friend, co-worker, or peer who has a shared experience—but the importance of the role of a caring guide, advisor, or compassionate ear can't be overstated. Peer support has been shown to be a powerful aspect of recovery or endurance of medical challenges. For example, millions of family members caring for a loved one who has dementia have turned to the Alzheimer's Society for guidance and support. Military members living with PTSD have established massive peer-support networks that have become lifelines for countless veterans. Belonging to a group where members come together to confront mutual challenges is invaluable.

The difference between living on the brink of burnout and becoming burned out can be the community you build around you. They are the watch-people who stand on guard for you. The time to build your community is always now—so it's there for you when you're in need. The people who emerged stronger from the pandemic, those who were most resilient, were those who could access an array of allies who were willing to help them in ways both big and small. They were also the ones who others called on in return. They experienced the validation and reassurance that comes from being seen to be valuable to others.

Throughout the last three years, I've occasionally found myself feeling like I was at the end of the road, professionally speaking. It took someone in my supportive community to show me that I was just at a bend, rather than the end. I have a visceral sense of belonging to an extraordinary community of purpose-driven people. My community is ever growing—but I need to keep making deposits into the community account. So here's my question for you: How are you earning the fellowship and support of the people who will be there to sustain you, if you find yourself on the brink, and support you so you don't go over the edge?

Feeling safe means always having people who will be there to strengthen you when you're not strong. And that means you need to be there to strengthen them when you *are* strong. In sunny times prepare for storms. In stormy times, prepare for sunshine. At all times, be prepared for a change of weather. Remember: there is no such thing as bad weather, just inappropriate clothing.

THE QUICK WIN

In her post-burnout life, Diane has had to recalibrate her drive to be "everywhere" and smack down her FOMO tendencies. "It hasn't been easy," she shares. "But I knew I'd end up in the very same place if I didn't make some changes. I instituted what I call my yearly 'state of the union,' where I take a few hours to ask myself whether I'm living up to my values. This requires time, as I must recollect and write them down and then honestly reflect on whether I've lived up to them, personally and professionally. My family comes first, but my schedule didn't always ensure I was present for them. Because of my state of the unions, I've radically changed my work-life balance. I've upped my fitness. I've stopped the crazy weekends, where I felt I had to get every house chore done.

"My team at work has also played a role in helping me find more balance. As a lone practitioner in a private practice, I was only responsible for myself and my patients. Now, I have a product to deliver and a team that is depending on me on so many levels. That meant I had to let go of so many other things I'd been doing for years—some of which I was terrified to let go of. Doing so made me available for what means the most to me now."

What steps can you take to protect yourself against burnout? If you're experiencing burnout, what changes, plans, or system adjustments can you make to restore your vitality? How can you support people on the brink of burnout so they can achieve the breakthroughs they're looking for?

14

Recognize That Stress Attacks Us All—Even the Champions

ON JANUARY 19, 2022, together with her co-host Corey Hirsch, Diane interviewed Kevin Love on her podcast *Blindsided*. Kevin is a basketball player for the Miami Heat and won an NBA championship with the Cleveland Cavaliers in 2016. He's also one of the most prominent professional athletes to speak out about his struggles with mental illness. His article for the *Players' Tribune*, "Everyone Is Going Through Something," struck a chord. It helped a lot of people and athletes to open up.

On the podcast, Kevin shared the details of his life with Diane and Corey. Kevin was mentored by his father from an early age to play elite-level basketball. His father had played for the NBA and exposed Kevin to countless hours of videos of the basketball greats from different eras.

Kevin came from a family of high achievers. His uncle was a founding member of the Beach Boys, his aunt was a triathlete, and his mother was a nurse. He was driven by high expectations—both those he put on himself and the ones he felt were imposed on him. Growing up in a small town in Oregon, Kevin experienced anxiety at a young age but didn't have the resources to help him address it. (Today, he takes anxiety medication and sees two therapists to deal with his anxiety symptoms. He's grateful to be able to afford the treatment.)

Kevin describes his anxiety as a low-level threat that something could go wrong at any time—it clings to him at all times like a weighted vest. But it became a driving force in his life because he thought he could "achieve himself out of it." He used the anxiety as a fuel, but it also drained his energy as he struggled to continually maintain a facade of toughness and confidence. Still, he worried that if his teammates and coaches discovered this, they might lose faith in him. He found it impossible to be vulnerable and to speak his truth. As he puts it, he just couldn't keep up with playing the character of Kevin Love.

Even though Kevin joined the NBA at nineteen, he started seeing a therapist only in his late twenties, after a very public panic attack forced him to seek help. He recalls those years as a very dark time in his life. He felt trapped in a "just endure" mentality that stopped him from feeling compassion for himself or asking for help. Since then, he has learned a completely new way of thinking. He now believes that "nothing haunts us like the things we don't say. You must speak your truth—you disarm people when you do that."

On November 5, 2017, Kevin experienced a panic attack during a game, in front of twenty-three thousand people. The intensity of the panic caused him to flee; he ran from the court to the safety of the team's locker room. He recalls feeling so ashamed, he found it difficult to make eye contact with anyone. He also remembers feeling like he was choking, as if there was a blockage in his windpipe, and—like so many others' experience in the midst of a panic attack—thinking that he was dying. Soon after, he was assessed at the Cleveland Clinic and learned he was fine—at least from a physical standpoint.

Kevin's panic attack was so terrifying he decided he would do anything to get better. He began writing about it in a journal, which was deeply therapeutic. He also shared his experience with others and found them to be highly supportive. Kevin now believes that people are tribal beings and that those who experience anxiety and depression must form a community to support one another.

Following the panic attack, Kevin continued to feel that people were looking at him and judging him. He created false narratives and shut himself off from others. He believes that this was a difficult but necessary path of self-acceptance—that he had to "go through it to grow through it." Quoting Steve Jobs, Kevin says, "You can't connect the dots looking forward; you can only connect them looking backwards." He is thankful for the experience but wishes he could go back and enjoy his time in the game more. He has learned that you shouldn't be more concerned with tomorrow's tribulations than yesterday's triumphs. (However, Kevin understands that that's just the way his brain is wired.)

In 2018, he started the Kevin Love Fund to help others by providing tools and research to deal with the stigma of anxiety and depression. He is proud of his fund's educational curriculum, which models vulnerability and other forms of emotional learning. To date, thousands of teenagers and hundreds of teachers have been positively affected by Kevin's experience, resilience, and perseverance.

Pressure and Panic Are Conjoined Twins

Anyone can experience a panic attack. While most panic attacks are associated with a mental illness, such as panic disorder, depression, or bipolar disorder, about 30 percent of the time the sufferer has no psychiatric disorder. Diane explains: "A panic attack can be provoked by a highly distressing thought or situation or occur seemingly out of the blue. Panic disorder is a mental illness characterized by repeated, un-cued (unexpected) panic attacks and persistent fears that follow an attack, including fear of having another attack, worry about the consequences of the attack (e.g., having a heart attack or dying), or changes in behaviour, such as avoidance of situations, all of which negatively impact functioning. When you have a panic attack, your anxiety level goes from zero to a hundred in a matter of moments, associated with a range of physical (e.g., racing heart, sweating, trembling) and emotional (e.g., fear of dying, feeling unreal) symptoms. Panic symptoms usually peak in about ten minutes and then slowly subside, but the impact, in terms of persistent worries, can last for much longer."

As Kevin demonstrated, if you don't know what a panic attack is, it's impossible to control it. Being able to recognize the symptoms of subsequent attacks enables you to deal with them, whether it's something you can manage yourself or by seeking professional help. More importantly, they're unlikely to go away on their own, so if you're struggling with repeated panic attacks or chronic anxiety, reaching out to a professional is a major step in helping you to regain your sense of control.

Pressure and panic are conjoined twins. Even the most stoic individual will yield to extreme pressure, if only for a moment. Diane and I experience flashes of anxiety multiple times a week. When you're up to big things, big things can go wrong. When you're confronted with problems you've never had to face before, you can feel like your life is being threatened—because at some level it is. Your primitive brain, the amygdala, doesn't understand the difference between a real threat and an imagined one. In the throes of panic, it can seem like an email or a word can be deadly.

According to a 2021 study by the Centers for Disease Control and Prevention, 41.5 percent of adults reported "recent symptoms of an anxiety or depressive disorder," an increase from an already high baseline of 36.4 percent just months before. Increasingly, anxiety is becoming our default mental state. That means we have to work even harder to get back to homeostasis. Homeostasis is a self-regulating process by which we maintain internal equilibrium while adjusting to external conditions. It is dynamic and different for each person, depending on their mindset, physiology, and life situations.

11 Stress Relief Techniques

Here are eleven ways to deal with extreme stress:

1 Prepare for panic. Or, better yet, prepare not to panic—by knowing your anxiety triggers and your early panic symptoms. If you recognize the experience as an extreme stress moment (ESM), you can put your panic prevention strategy into motion. Sometimes ESMs last mere moments, and sometimes they persist. When Diane speaks to her patients, she refers to these times as "pre-panic." She adds, "You're not in a full panic attack—it's more vague and not yet fully defined. But if you recognize the signs and symptoms, you can take steps to prevent panic or mitigate the severity." In my case, my mouth goes dry and I break into a cold sweat. It usually happens when I lose my way through a speech, or I realize I've made a really

bad investment, or someone tells me that I've offended them. I should be able to handle all those situations with aplomb but they can still bring me to my knees—for an instant. Then, I engage my panic prevention strategies, as I share below.

2 Use positive self-talk. When you're experiencing an ESM, acknowledge it aloud like a mantra: "I'm just having an ESM. It will pass quickly. It's all in my mind. I can control this. I've been here before. I'm safe."

3 Oxygenate. Breathe evenly, but not too deeply. It's critical that you do not hold your breath. Diane adds, "People don't realize they're holding their breath when they panic, but it's a panic trigger. It's all but impossible to panic if you maintain a regular, even breathing pattern."

4 Hydrate, Meditate, Concentrate, Activate (HMCA). Hydrate: drink a glass of water. Meditate: still your mind. Concentrate: shift your focus to something else. Activate: get moving, by taking a vigorous walk.

5 Tell someone you trust. If you know the cause, share it with them. Listen to yourself speak. Listen to what they say to you. Just be with the words. Know that talking out loud helps you make sense of the storm in your head.

6 Look ahead. Remind yourself that you can handle whatever is in front of you, just like you have throughout your life—but confront the fact that you need help.

7 Have compassion for yourself. Don't lambaste or be angry with yourself. Treat yourself like someone you love.

8 Avoid making far-reaching decisions until the ESM has passed. Diane adds, "This is a rule to follow for all emotional crises. If you're struggling with depression, anxiety, or

another acute mental illness, such that you're not functioning optimally, it's not the right time to make life-altering decisions. I urge my patients not to impulsively plan a move, get married or divorced, or take any other major life decision if they're not making that choice with their brain intact. Cognition (memory, concentration, executive functioning) is significantly impacted by mental illness, especially if it's severe."

9. Reflect on the benefits. Post-ESM, reflect on what you learned from the experience because that will reduce its power over you. Begin with the phrase, "It was the best thing that happened to me because..." Find a reason to complete that statement and believe it. Remember your lessons learned the next time.

10. Adjust your lifestyle. Work to identify and slowly employ lifestyle changes that will help you to achieve and maintain homeostasis and restore your inner equilibrium. Do the things that are good for you and make you feel good. Remind yourself of your power to recover and reinvent yourself. Diane adds, "Rome wasn't built in a day. Step one is considering changes that might help, like ensuring you get thirty minutes of mild-to-moderate physical activity daily, take your breaks, and turn off your phone after work hours. Make a list of what needs to change and then develop a plan to introduce those changes, but not all at once. Take little bites. Trying to eat the whole elephant at once is impossible, so people give up."

11. Get professional help. If the ESM persists or you're experiencing repeated panic attacks, consult a mental health professional—or doctor, nurse practitioner, or psychologist.

If you're in the presence of someone experiencing an ESM, express your empathy with them. Use phrases like, "I know this feels awful but I also know it will pass," or "I feel your anxiety, and we'll work it out together," or "I'm here for you through this difficult time," or "I can see how that would really worry you, and I can also see that it will get resolved," or "I've been where you are and I know you'll get through it, too."

Make Others Feel Safe When You Are Scared

The greatest compliment that anyone can pay you is to turn to you in their ESM. If you become known as the person that soothes others' fears, you will be a walking safe zone for them. In the year that Diane and I wrote this book together, we became safe zones for each other. Every week, we would share our crises with each other and walk each other off the ledge. Ironically, writing the book was a major cause of my own ESMs, especially when I was tired or frustrated by my own procrastination. Talking with Diane about it was both a source of contentment and therapy. I can tell you that everything we're sharing with you in this book works—I'm living proof. Phew!

No matter who you are—whatever your function or position—you're either a source of safety or you're cause for concern. You're reinforcing people's belief in themselves, their environment, and their future, or you're amplifying their alarm. It's binary.

So, who are you? Would people choose to have you in their foxhole? Or are they glad when you're not there? Are the five to ten feet around you a place where people can breathe easier? Or are you a walking danger zone? How do you know? Are people coming to you with problems to be solved? Do they seek out your counsel? Do they call you in a crisis? Are they acknowledging your contribution? Are they relaxed in your presence?

Making others feel safe when you are scared is one of the best ways to make yourself feel safe. It requires the ability to transcend your fears about yourself so you can comfort others. You'll discover that helping others increases your sense of agency. Often, by verbalizing ways of addressing the problem, you find the solution for yourself. What's more, you elicit valuable insights from others that provide you with new ways to move forward.

Depending on the situation, you may have to play the role of protector, inspirer, catalyst, coach, wing-person, confidante, servant, or listener-in-chief. The more you function effectively in a particular role, the more others will identify it as one of your strengths. You'll become more confident, and it will become infinitely easier to sustain the required behaviour. That's because you'll have rewired your brain using good neuroplasticity—now you own that role!

It's OK to acknowledge your fear. Diane calls vulnerability a leadership superpower. It makes you real, relatable, and even aspirational. It's the actions that make the difference. The best way to master fear is to run toward it and through it.

More importantly, being helpful, soothing fear, or providing thoughtful guidance isn't the same as taking over, fixing the problem, or telling someone what to do. Leaders shouldn't be in the business of solving every challenge. Having the answer to every problem is an impossible weight to bear. Great leaders empower their team members to find their own solutions, whether it's an interpersonal conflict, a work-related crisis, or a personal health issue. This approach builds resilience, confidence, and ownership of the win. Diane describes her role as a psychiatrist as an educated, experienced navigator. Her patients captain their own ship.

THE QUICK WIN

Through their *Blindsided* podcast, Diane and her co-host, Corey Hirsch, hope to destigmatize mental illness through the stories of well-known, respected, and revered elite athletes. By sharing their stories and painful journeys, they hope others will feel less alone and be more likely to reach out for help. In her other roles, Diane has witnessed the power of leadership vulnerability in many more contexts. "I remember attending a meeting a few years ago where one of the company's most senior leaders told his entire team, hundreds of people during a virtual town hall, that he suffered from panic disorder. As I listened to his brave disclosure, I watched the meeting chat at the side of my screen explode with kind, thoughtful, appreciative, and moving comments. It was heartwarming and inspirational. As a leader, I've learned that sharing my feelings, admitting my mistakes, and being myself makes my team feel safer and more willing to reach out when they need help."

In your next extreme stress moment, utilize one of the eleven ways we've outlined to regain your equilibrium. And watch out for colleagues' ESMs. Help them reclaim their homeostasis. Then check in on them to ensure they're sustaining their recovery.

15

Drink the FGA (Forgiveness, Gratitude, Agency) Tonic

FEAR, ANXIETY, uncertainty, doubt, apathy, resentment, upset, anger, guilt, and suspicion. These are all emotions that drain you of well-being. They suck the lifeblood out of you. They make you miserable. They are pro-inflammatory. They negatively impact your brain function and structure. As we described in chapter five, the amygdala of a chronically depressed or anxious brain is always screaming at the hypothalamus, "This is an emergency!" because it constantly feels under attack, even if there isn't an obvious threat. As a result, the HPAA axis is constantly in overdrive, desperately trying to get the stressed-out brain to calm down. Cortisol levels stay high and don't settle back to normal because the threat never fully resolves, leaving the brain vulnerable.

Chronically high levels of cortisol can have devastating effects on a depressed or anxious brain because, eventually, in situations of prolonged and severe stress, the brain starts to ignore cortisol. It's like the boy who cried wolf: the brain stops reacting to the amygdala's cries for help as brain cells become increasingly insensitive to cortisol, much like how chronically high levels of insulin lead to insulin insensitivity in type 2 diabetics. Over time, cortisol becomes less effective at preventing inflammation and may in fact start to cause or worsen inflammation.

Anxiety or depression-inducing emotions need to be replaced by emotions that nurture and replenish you. Give yourself and everyone around you the tonic of FGA: forgiveness, gratitude, and agency.

Forgiveness

Forgiveness doesn't mean forgetting. Forgiveness means deciding to give up the anger, guilt, or resentment we feel, toward ourselves or someone else, for a wrongdoing. "We can't change what has happened, but we can change the power a negative experience has over our life," Diane shares. "There's a pervasive belief that we forgive to help the wrongdoer feel better, but I've learned that I'm the person who benefits most from forgiving. It's difficult to forgive sometimes, but it frees me from the weight of those negative emotions. Hate, anger, resentment—they all rot the vessel they're in. They poison my spirit. When I let those feelings go, I shed an unwanted burden." Most importantly, forgiveness gives us the ability to move forward free from the terrible toll those emotions take. We may be tempted to punish ourselves for a perceived mess-up by constantly

Angry, guilty, or resentful people are never sources of safety.

castigating ourselves, but that mindset doesn't serve us. It just inflames our feelings of inadequacy or worthlessness. If you cannot forgive, you end up taking out your anger on people who had nothing to do with the incident in the first place. Angry, guilty, or resentful people are never sources of safety.

Diane and I are repelled by the weaponization of language. We believe it harms communities. We need to forgive people their faux pas if their intentions are good. Be a coach, not a judge. In a world where there are too many political, religious, racial, and cultural divides, we need more allies. We must lift each other up, rather than denigrating and pushing people away. Those who wish to be an ally, who want to learn, and who were raised in a time of different sensitivities clam up because they're terrified to say the wrong thing. A safe environment means enabling people to communicate without fear of being condemned or cancelled. The decision to forgive belongs to the person who is wronged, but, without a doubt, it benefits both parties.

Gratitude

Gratitude is not just being thankful but also being ready to show appreciation and to return kindness. It's immunity against complacency or entitlement. It saves you from lamenting what you don't have so you can love what you do. It heightens your joy because every gift is savoured like the grace it is. Lack of gratitude is a one-way ticket to unhappiness because nothing is enough—even for those who have more than enough.

Agency

Agency means that you have the power to prevail. You can influence what happens next. You can make an important difference. You're an originator, not a spectator. When Diane feels anxious, she thinks: *This feels crappy but this is the worst that it gets. I'm coming out the other side. I always do.* Diane has worries like everyone else, but she's learned that by acknowledging her feelings, she immediately feels more powerful and certain she can overcome them. "Just by articulating how I feel, I experience a sense of relief," she shares. Critically, there is a difference between experiencing normal worries and being severely anxious or depressed. When chronic fear, sadness, hopelessness, and worthlessness become a state of being, that's when to seek professional help.

When you exercise your agency, you encourage others to express their agency. You nudge them into saying or doing things that otherwise would have intimidated them into inertia. Every time you celebrate activity and try new things, irrespective of outcome, another deposit in the trust account is made.

THE QUICK WIN

Diane's childhood was not as overtly chaotic as mine, but it wasn't an oasis of calm cohesiveness, either. "Both of my parents were married three times," she shares. "Neither one was as involved as they should have been, but at least my mother was physically present. By that I mean she lived in the same house. I refer to myself as having been a feral child. For years, I felt angry because I had never been parented. It's extremely difficult to learn to be an adult when you are one, and I'm eternally grateful for those who gave me the grace to find my way. Then I saw the impact of the same kind of chronic anger and resentment, in family members, friends, and patients who couldn't forgive and let go. It's not a good look, inside or out. I realized I had to forgive my parents, for me. They didn't ask for forgiveness—one of them never would—but for my own well-being, it was an essential, life-altering step."

In her book *This Is Depression*, Diane writes of her belief that some of the greatest gifts in life are the gifts we give ourselves. For her, one of those gifts is forgiveness. "Getting to forgiveness can take time—especially for something that was really hurtful. And I might not be able to forget the pain the transgression caused, but I know that if I can find forgiveness, invariably I feel better, like a weight has been lifted off my shoulders."

Try to think about someone you've been unable to forgive. It might not be the right time yet, but consider what it would feel like to unburden yourself of the weight of that anger and resentment. If forgiveness has always been a challenge for you, first seek to forgive smaller infractions—little resentments that built up over time.

16

Know That Trust Is the Most Valuable Thing You Can Give

THE MOST EMPOWERING thing that anyone can say is "I trust you." It is the ultimate acknowledgement of your worth and validation of your status. As a professional speaker, when I hear a client say those three magic words to me, I feel free to be me. I open up. I try new approaches. I talk with a confidence that would never be possible if I felt second-guessed or micromanaged. The greater the consequences, the more powerful trust becomes. If others declare their trust in you, you become more likely to trust yourself. To paraphrase Van Morrison, have you told someone lately that you trust them?

On the other hand, the moment you feel entitled to someone else's trust, you begin losing it. Trust requires daily deposits of effort, love, and results. Relationships don't end because of the great betrayal. They end because of lack of effort. The enemy of trust is complacency—whatever you take for granted, you eventually lose.

Every decision tilts toward trust. It entails a choice between what you believe in and what you don't. Every day, you're making decisions based on your interpretation of the options available to you—especially the human ones.

What motivated you to read this book? Was it the title? Did you recognize Diane's or my name? Have you read some of our previous work? Was it recommended by people in your network? Whatever it was, it gave you a reason to trust us. It caused you to take a risk with your money, time, attention, and energy.

Diane's expressed trust in my ability to create *You Belong Here* with her sustained me during the inevitable moments of self-doubt that come with any worthwhile endeavour. On the one hand, I wanted to honour her trust. On the other, I was going to do everything to not lose it. It simply wasn't an option.

How many people trust you to come through for them in the most important ways? And how many people do you trust to come through for you in the most important ways? The answer is the same for both questions: more than you think.

You are a vital link in the relationship chain. You are either strengthening people's willingness to trust others or you are eroding it. We become the sum of all our experiences. I'm writing these words because of the deposits in the trust account by all my stakeholders over a lifetime. I'm fortunate that many more people invested than withheld their trust from me. In turn, trusting others is my default position. When I meet you, you automatically have my trust, not because I am naive, but because I know that's the best way to earn *your* trust.

There is a direct correlation between the willingness to trust and success, as measured in education and income. According to a 2020 global Pew Research study, the higher the level of education and income, the greater the willingness to trust. Interestingly, Canadians are more willing to trust than Americans: 71 percent of Canadians say most people can be trusted, versus only 58 percent of Americans. In both Canada and America, those under thirty are less willing to trust versus those over fifty—by a wide margin. I take that fact as positive news. It suggests that life experience generates trust. So, whatever your demographic, do your due diligence but begin trusting people now.

Trust Always Means Risk

If you trust people, you run the risk of loss, disappointment, distress, or even humiliation. But if you don't trust people, you run the risk of achieving nothing. You shut yourself off from possibility. You eliminate opportunity at the source. Trust comes with a severe hazard warning—it is essential to success and happiness, and it has a high probability of pain and failure. At some point, even the most trustworthy people will let you down, despite their best intentions. They will change course. They will leave. They will make mistakes. They will switch their trust to someone else. Prepare yourself for those moments and carry on.

When you lose your trust in someone, try to forgive them quickly, especially if you still have to coexist with them. Learn from your experience with them and manage your

Grudges grind you down.

expectations accordingly. Shed the load of resentment, disillusionment, or anger that weighs you down. No one is at their best when they're nursing a grievance. The danger is that they take their frustration out on people that had nothing to do with the grievance in the first place. As Will Smith said, "Hurt people hurt people."

The more you feel an emotion, the more habituated you become to feeling that emotion. Don't let the loss-of-trust event become an entrenched state of mind. Grudges grind you down. We all have to work with people with whom we didn't choose to work. Letting go of the past is the key to grabbing hold of the future. Reframe the experience in your mind. Regard it as something that was meant to happen because it did. Accept it as fact just like you accept gravity. And act accordingly.

When *you* let someone else down, immediately acknowledge your culpability. Express your contrition. Trust means always having to say you're sorry—like you mean it. An authentic apology can restore someone's trust in you immediately. Lack of contrition, on the other hand, will calcify the injury. There is a big difference between saying, "my apologies," and "I'm so sorry." The first is a passive expression of the bare minimum. The second is a heartfelt declaration of shared pain. Often, an authentic apology is all that is required to set the relationship back on track. If you accept that you're wrong, you can make it right. Resist the temptation to justify why you acted wrongly. An apology is better without the explanation. "I'm sorry but..." does not pave the path to forgiveness.

THE QUICK WIN

Just like forgiveness can take time and doesn't always include forgetting, rebuilding trust takes time and might never be fully restored. It can take years to build a trusting business relationship and seconds to destroy it, with an ill-considered post; a thoughtless, insensitive comment; or, worse, a long, detailed, angry email.

Many years ago, following an impulsive and unpleasant communication, Diane promised herself that she would never send an angry email on the same day it was written. She shares, "I laid down the 24-hour law after learning that emails are not the same as other forms of communication. You can't take them back, they're instant, and you can't properly share your feelings, or any nuances, the way you can on the phone or in person. And email doesn't do sarcasm well. Invariably, if I give myself some time for sober second thought, I scrap the whole message and send nothing, or send one with an entirely different tone." Once you've sent an inflammatory message, it can reverberate for days or maybe even forever (which, by the way, should be considered for every kind of communication). Don't risk harming your brand, your trust, and your team by impulsive communication. Take every opportunity to make a deposit into the trust account, because if you do fail to follow the 24-hour law, it's valuable to have built up some serious equity.

Over the next week, tell your most important stakeholders how much you trust them because of the extraordinary contribution they've made to you personally and professionally. And earn others' trust by being so remarkable that they trust you even more to exceed their expectations in the future.

17

Build Belonging by Being Whole in a Splintered Reality

TODAY, YOU WILL PLAY multiple roles on the stage called Your Life. You will be a professional, a parent, a partner, a psychologist, an advisor, a confessor, a pioneer, a leader, a follower, a truth-teller, a pretender, a friend, a reader, a listener, a healer, or a rescuer—take your pick. You will play these roles either intentionally or mindlessly. You will be aware of your impact or blind to it. You will feel good about your performance or worried that it's not good enough at all. You will have invested in your well-being or amplified your angst. Most importantly, you will have increased your followership or alienated your allies. There is no middle ground.

Either you're growing your community or you're eroding it. It can be an acute spike in members or a gradual change, but it's never static.

Overlaying your multiple roles are the many ways in which you communicate: in person, by phone, synchronously online through video or chat, or asynchronously through text or email. Each medium is an integral expression of who you are and what you represent to others. For example, if you are an effective face-to-face communicator but an ineffectual virtual presenter, you will diminish your stature with others. If you are compelling one-to-one but shaky one-to-many, you will lose the opportunity to win your share of others' minds. The law of recency states that we are often only as good as our last conversation or presentation to others.

The Naked-You versus the Dressed-You

Adaptive navigation by role and medium is vital. Versatility is an essential skill. Strategies and tactics change from situation to situation. The way you engage your clients and employees may be very different from the way you engage with your family. Your approach should be guided by function or circumstance. Your style may shift based on your audience, but your central character must be constant. Think of it like the naked-you versus the dressed-you. The naked-you is always the same (give or take variation by weight and age). The dressed-you is dramatically different depending on the clothes you've donned for the occasion.

Integrity is the naked-you. It's what remains after everything else has been stripped away. It's what expresses itself in crises and clutch moments. You can mask anything, but integrity will shine through. It's the truth you tell, the promises you follow through on, the stands you take. A lack of integrity leads to the collapse of everything else. Without it, nothing ends up working.

Just like you, over our careers, Diane and I have worked with people who lack integrity. We call them Swiss Cheese People—they have holes in their character. It's always a gut punch when you discover their deficits. It's usually when they've won your confidence. They've earned your faith. They've made you dependent on them. They've entered your inner sanctum. They've weaponized your belief in them against you. Your hurt or sense of betrayal is directly proportional to the trust you've placed in them.

Today, Diane and I choose our social and professional partners based on their integrity. We do our due diligence as best we can. We listen for their values in the stories they share. We watch for inconsistencies. We've discovered that people will tell you who they are if you pay enough attention to what they tell you. If they call others "idiots," justify unjustifiable actions, or share their contempt or disrespect for people, they are communicating their lack of integrity.

When you hear the things you don't want to hear, don't lie to yourself. Don't look for ways to rationalize what you plainly see. Learn from the people who've conned you but don't allow them to confiscate your faith in others. At the same time, talk and act with others like they've been let down by someone else, because chances are they have. If you always act like you need to earn and re-earn others' trust, you're likely to do the right thing.

Silence Isn't Golden—It Can Be Toxic

Silence is malpractice when others expect and need to hear from you. Lack of response can be worse than even a cursory reply. In the absence of feedback, silence prompts people to

If you always act like you need to earn others' trust, you're likely to do the right thing.

fill the void with their own speculation, creating unnecessary doubt and fuelling mistrust. You can deal with the devil you know. It's the not knowing that's debilitating. Integrity means always saying what needs to be said, otherwise you will be sorry someday. Life's a circle and what goes around comes around.

Stake your claim early. In every meeting, let people know where you stand sooner rather than later—especially if you're a leader or a senior member of the team. I'm coaching a leader of a large energy equipment manufacturer. Let's call him Sam. Sam is exquisitely talented but he's also reticent to express himself until he knows which way the wind is blowing. So, he hangs back until he believes it's safe to talk—usually in the closing stages of a meeting. As a result, his people or outside constituents don't know what he's thinking. That means they can't leverage his insights to sharpen their own. Because people wait for him to speak, there are often conversational breakdowns where they dance around critical issues. I counselled Sam to express his opinion early, not as a fait accompli, but as an invitation to others to weigh in.

We're all fallible. Just because someone lets you down doesn't mean that they lack integrity. Give people a chance. And then another. Maybe even another. But if the lapses become patterns, distance yourself. You may still have to work with these people, but you know not to admit them to your inner sanctum. Don't give up on them. They may simply be the victims of their own blind spots—these are aspects of their character that you can see but they cannot. Endeavour to share your insights with them. You never know when your communication will make a difference. But don't be disappointed when it doesn't.

1. **Live Your Code of Values**
2. **Be Whole**
3. **Be Consistent across Your Roles and Mediums of Communication**
4. **Say It, Then Do It**
5. **Be in Service to Others**

THE 5 FACETS OF FAITHWORTHINESS

BEING TRUSTWORTHY MEANS that people can depend on you. Being faithworthy means that people can believe in you. Trustworthiness is table stakes. It means that people don't have to worry about your performance. Faithworthiness is a game changer. It means that people are uplifted by your presence. You are proof that they can win, and a safe harbour when they don't.

Here is a five-point integrity checklist to evaluate your faithworthiness. Each point is a perpetual work in progress.

1. Live Your Code of Values

Do you know your top five values—in order of priority? Most people cannot tell you what theirs are. And if you don't know what they are, you'll only live them by accident. Intentionally living your code is the surest route to a life of integrity and no regrets. Mine are: being fully utilized, making a difference, connecting with others, loving life, being successful. Diane's are: compassion, happiness, knowledge, integrity, responsibility, humour, kindness, and love.

2. Be Whole

Whole means entire, unified, complete, and undiminished. Are you fully expressing your power? Or are you withholding your contribution? How much of you is going unused? Are you being worthy of your gifts? Are you being true to you? Are you consciously seeking self-actualization? I'm always in a state of tension around being whole, but I've made peace with it. It pulls me forward. Writing this book with Diane is one of the ways I'm being whole.

3. Be Consistent across Your Roles and Mediums of Communication

Champions perform at levels of excellence that they never fall below. They honour the standards they set for themselves by preparing for them. As Archilochus, an ancient Greek poet, said, "We don't rise to the level of our expectations, we fall to the level of our training." Excellence takes practice. Practice means repeated performance or systematic exercise for the purpose of acquiring skill or proficiency. That's how you build consistency, and it's consistency that builds loyalty and belonging.

4. Say It, Then Do It

How close are your actions to your commitments? If you give someone your word, can they take you at it? When all is said and done, more is said than done. Simply following through on promises will brand you as a person of integrity. But don't just under-promise and over-deliver. Make a bold promise and then find a way to deliver it—to the benefit of everyone around you.

5. Be in Service to Others

Martin Luther King Jr. said, "Everybody can be great because anybody can serve." Diane and I created *You Belong Here* to empower you with a sense of safety while you take bold risks and win. We are engaging in "altruism at a profit"—we want to cause maximum good while we advance our personal agendas. First, we serve. Then, we win. We're only as good as the difference we make.

I

Creating Belonging in a Hybrid World

III

Owning Your Power

II

Growing Enriching Relationships

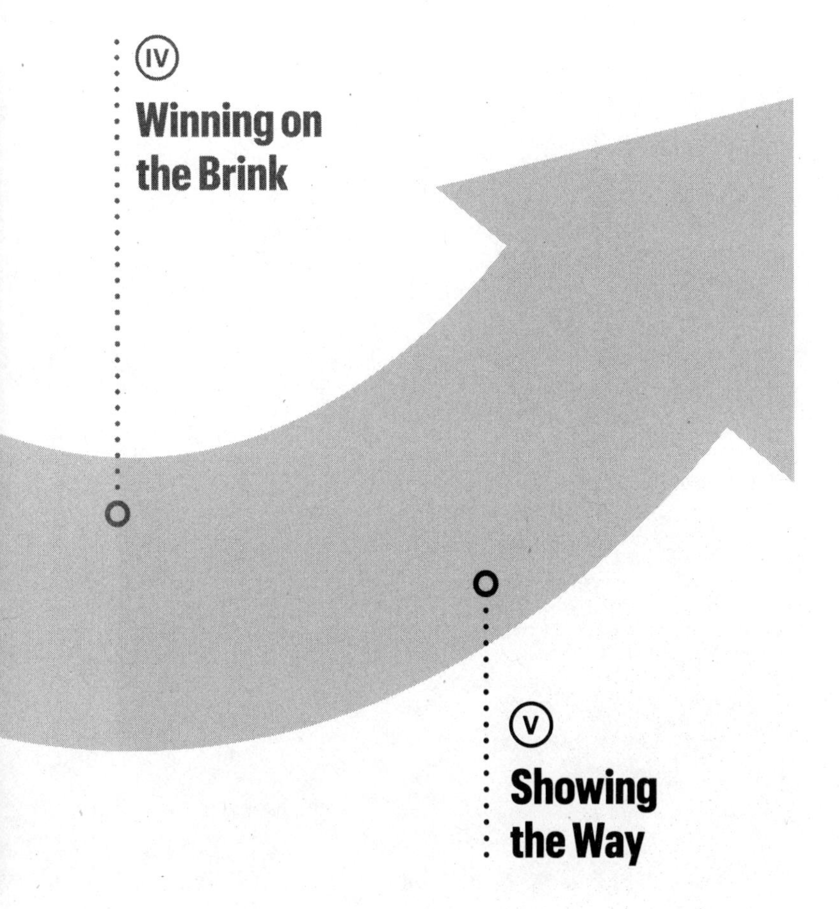
IV
Winning on the Brink
V
Showing the Way

PART V

SHOWING THE WAY

18

Understand That Resilience Can Be Reproduced

EVERY DAY, I watch Volodymyr Zelensky rally the world to his country's cause. I watch him captivate global audiences with his Churchillian calls to action. I see him charm global politicians with his humility and humanity. I marvel at his stamina as he criss-crosses the planet to broadcast his message through every outlet available to him.

As I have felt overwhelmed or defeated by my micro-issues, I think of Zelensky. I wonder what it must be like waking up every morning to confront an enemy hellbent on wiping out your existence. Then, I harness my inner Zelensky, and I cowboy up to take on my issue du jour. By reproducing even a fraction of Zelensky's resilience, I multiply my own. Most of the time, simply addressing the issue helps solve it. In turn, my daily resolve strengthens the resolve of the people with whom I communicate. And they in turn cascade their stick-to-it-ness to all their stakeholders.

If one person can, another person can, too. Courage is contagious. We're all sitting on the resilience teeter-totter. It can tilt toward capitulation or toward command, depending on the emphasis applied to either end. Life is a game of ounces. One extra ounce of emphasis at either end can mean the difference between winning and whining.

The best part of resilience is that it can be built—both individually and collectively. This is because the brain is constantly wiring and rewiring. Remember that epigenetics means that life experiences can actually change brain structure and function and how your genes are transcribed.

Genes make proteins, enzymes, and other chemicals that govern the inner workings of the body. Life experiences, therefore, change what chemicals are produced in the body. As you change your behaviour, you're also changing your genome. Whatever behaviours brought you to this point, you can intentionally change them to create your best internal chemistry in the future.

Every person that you have ever met has inscribed their impact on your genes. They have helped make you who you are today. Something as innocuous as a conversation with a cashier in a checkout line can leave its mark on you at the deepest level. At a more intimate level, when someone close to you leaves or passes on, celebrate what you have achieved together. Take stock and record their valuable contribution to your evolution because your interactions with them have literally shaped who you are, at a cellular level. At the same time, know that you are continuously leaving your mark on others.

You're either making them feel safe and like they belong, or you're a threat and a source of stress.

Ichi-go ichi-e is the most meaningful Japanese proverb to me. It literally means "one life, one meeting." It is inspired by the Japanese tea ceremony, which practices a philosophy that each tea ceremony shall be hosted as though it is a once-in-a-lifetime occasion. The belief is that a meeting of this nature will create such a connection between the guests that their relationship with one another and those in their social networks will be transformed thereafter. Japanese tea ceremonies are frequently held with business and government negotiations to connect guests and form the foundation of a trustful community. Likewise, hosts and guests of Japanese restaurants enjoy each morsel of food and sip of drink together as though it is the last banquet of their lives. This communicates the value of enjoying food and appreciating the occasion of dining with others.

If you approach every encounter with another person in an *ichi-go ichi-e* frame of mind, you'll transform both yourself and the other person with your engagement.

Grief Is the Price We Pay for Love

We cannot control everything that happens to us, but we can control how we respond to what happens to us. That's because we can control our own thoughts, feelings, and behaviours. There are random events. Bad things do happen to good people. In those moments, we need to focus on our personal discovery. We need to find the win—what are the solutions or lessons we can take from the experience? How can we turn things around? It hurts to lose your job, fail to make the sale, lose money on an investment, or experience a relationship breakdown. Naturally, there's a temptation to engage in self-pity, lambaste ourselves for our stupidity, or sink into a state of resignation and powerlessness. We might ask ourselves toxic questions: Why is this happening to me? How could they do this to me? Why would they leave me? How could I not see this coming?

Setbacks can injure our ego and deal a blow to our self-confidence. However, it's not uncommon to ultimately recognize that a setback or misfortune turned out to be at least a good thing, and sometimes the best possible thing. It's often important to thoughtfully reflect on why something happened, especially if it was unexpected. There is almost always a reason, so it's important to consider the circumstances and, if possible, recalibrate our approach for the future. There are situations that are completely beyond our control. But how we respond to them is definitely within our control. You're most likely to achieve a win from a loss if you have a solution-focused mind.

Of course loss hurts, especially the loss of someone we love. Even an *expected* loss, like the death of a loved one who is receiving palliative care, can still feel unendurable, like falling into the deepest, darkest well. As Queen Elizabeth so memorably shared in commemoration of the 9/11 victims, "Grief is the price we pay for love." Diane endured loss in her own unique way. "For me and almost everyone else, love is worth it," she says. "I've lost two people I adored, my maternal grandparents, but I found a way to soothe myself. Because I know that one-quarter of my DNA came from each of them, I know that they live on in me—I have them with me every single day. That's my 'science-y' way of comforting myself. We're each on our own journey through grief—your path through it will be unique to you, your loss, and your beliefs. But time does heal, sometimes imperfectly."

Diane has had many patients who experienced horrifying trauma and the most painful losses. "I've witnessed the most remarkable resilience and growth through the most devastating circumstances," she shares. "That fuelled my belief that resilience grows from weathering life's challenges. However, having a strong support system is essential—there's no shame in asking for help. Empathy has its limits, so if your family, friends, or colleagues are losing patience, that's a message to seek support from a professional.

"Obviously, there's also a major difference between a professional setback and the loss of a treasured loved one," Diane adds. "People are often uncomfortable when reaching out or speaking to a grieving person, but ignoring them and their loss can add to their pain for a couple of reasons. Your acknowledgement can give them the space to recover. Because they're grieving, they're not themselves, so it's reassuring to know their friends and workmates understand their loss. Additionally, they want to keep the rich memories of their loved one alive. There are no exact timelines for recovering from the death of someone we love, so resist the urge to share your opinions on that front."

We can take the good out of everything else in our life if we don't adjust to our losses and failures, however catastrophic they might be. Grievous losses can erode resilience, or they can grow it. The way I've framed my two-year struggle with clinical depression, which held me hostage from 1990 to 1992, is that it unleashed my talent as a writer and speaker. It empowered me to pursue a life of glorious self-actualization and international adventure. I can trace a direct line from the disease to this sentence. It was a miraculous gift. I wouldn't wish depression on anyone, nor would I ask to be depressed again. In fact, I spend my life working to ensure that I never experience another depression. Yet, those two years of living in the depths of despair ultimately built my resilience, my career, and so much of what I now hold dear.

Every step we take has a downstream effect of helping others—people we love, work with, or simply encounter through our days. As you master your nemesis or beat back your bogeyman, you're inspiring others to take control of themselves and beat back their own demons. Think about that consequence the next time you're tempted to throw in the towel or retreat from a situation you know you must take on.

Just Own It

The silver bullet of resilience comes with the simple realization that you own your recovery from the event that knocked you down. There may be multitudes of people who can help you, but ultimately, it's on you to spring back from the setback. The toughest part of the process is the adjustment period between loss and recovery, also known as the valley of the shadow of death. Navigating and overcoming the personal or professional challenge enables us to bask in the illuminating light of life. That's the essence of resilience—not just getting through something, but coming through with new strengths and a renewed (or new) belief in your own abilities.

Be aware of the seven stages of summoning resilience as you navigate your way toward recovery:

1. **Feeling the shock:** You suffer the gut punch of your loss or misfortune.

2. **Experiencing temporary immobility:** You are paralyzed by feelings of sadness, despair, bewilderment, or outrage.

3. **Processing your pain:** You ask yourself what this difficult event means to you and how it will impact your life going forward.

4. **Making real peace with your new reality:** You give yourself the grace and time that leads to acceptance of what has happened and what it means for your future.
5. **Resolving to recover:** You compassionately but firmly tell yourself, "I will recover," consciously confirming you're on the road to recovery.
6. **Making an action plan:** You prepare yourself to build a stronger, more resilient future based on what you've learned.
7. **Acting with conviction and the freedom of self-reinvention:** You take the necessary steps to realize your goals and ambition.

Sometimes, all seven stages can happen in a morning. Or sometimes, they can take much longer. Allow yourself the time to reflect and reset. Then re-engage with mojo. Resist the urge to set unrealistic timelines, but seek guidance from trusted advisors if you're feeling stuck. If you're hearing unsolicited feedback from those same trusted advisors that you seem stuck, listen to them and seek professional support, depending on the severity, from a coach, counsellor, or psychologist.

WD-40, the company behind the iconic brand of all-purpose degreasers, lubricants, and rust removal products, has crafted a "Maniac Pledge" that epitomizes the spirit of resilience ownership: "I'm responsible for taking action, asking questions, getting answers and making decisions. I won't wait for someone to tell me. If I need to know, I'm responsible for asking. I have no right to be offended that I didn't get this sooner. If I'm doing something others should know about, I'm responsible for telling them."

If you live the Maniac Pledge, you'll become a prolific purveyor of resilience to the enormous benefit of everyone around you.

Make Deposits into Your and Others' Health and Well-Being Accounts

Resilience is a skill set that pays big dividends. By increasing your own capacity to endure, you increase the capacity of your community to carry on. What begins as highly challenging becomes self-perpetuating with practice. If you prove that you can rise above your troubles, you're not tempted to let them sink you. The impossible becomes imminently and entirely possible.

You should never feel guilty about making your health and well-being the most important things in your life. You cannot positively influence other areas of your life if you haven't paid yourself first. And you cannot give what you haven't got. Every deposit in your health and well-being account is a payment you can make to others. And it keeps getting better—every payment you make to others enriches you even more. Watching another human being grow through our contribution is deeply satisfying. In AA, the core principle is to go to a group regularly—every week or even, for some, every day—so you can give and get support and acknowledgement to and from your fellow members. It's an altruistic give-to-get program, paying dividends to everyone.

The essence of most groups—AA, or Weight Watchers, or even book clubs—is to create a communal experience so you can compare, share, and learn together. Diane believes group therapy is an excellent therapeutic modality. "I've never had a patient who was initially excited by the prospect of group therapy. However, once they realized that everyone else has the same worries about confidentiality, they're more comfortable with the whole idea. While everyone in a psychotherapy group shares the common goal of learning new psychological skills, most importantly, groups create a family dynamic where differences provide unique perspectives."

Perspective is the key to self-realization. People who spend too much time by themselves can become strange. They start to believe that their internal reality represents actual reality. Without others' points of view, their own view becomes severely restricted. So get out there and meet people. For Diane and for me, that means attending industry association meetings, participating in pro bono causes, sitting on boards, or convening meetings with colleagues, clients, and friends. Simply travelling to new places where you're bound to bump into new people with new ideas is a way to share, compare, and learn.

Every place you give gives back at least twofold to you—even when you think your generosity is going unreciprocated. The truth is that you're building your giving-muscle irrespective of what others return to you. More often than not, you will be delighted by the surprising benefits of contribution. Even when her patients cannot work, Diane encourages them to volunteer. Giving with an open heart is a powerful investment in one's own sense of potency. You can always make a difference to someone.

There is a caveat here: you need to ensure that giving doesn't take over your life and lead to internal angst. You cannot care so much about others that it adversely impacts your own physical and mental health. Establishing your own priorities is a critical part of resilience. Just because someone is blood related, it doesn't mean that they should consume your heart and soul. People can spend their entire lives trying to be loved by someone who can't love them the way they should be loved. Or we can have people close to us who refuse to participate in their own rescue. We must do the most we can and then free ourselves of the burden that others refuse to carry for themselves.

It's Not about Chasing Happiness, It's about Being Happy While Chasing

Diane is a scientist. She believes that if we follow the science, we'll find solutions. But she also believes that science is being weaponized against us, which is having a serious impact on our health and sense of well-being. We're bombarded by bad news because bad news sells. The drama of politics means overplaying negativity by playing it over and over again. Algorithms decide what we see and hear in our news feeds. The noise is constant and discordant. If we're not vigilant, it's easy to get sucked into the media maelstrom.

In this context, intentional happiness is a survival skill. It's right up there with stamina, adaptability, and creativity. Happiness is a force multiplier. It magnifies the power of all other virtues. Without happiness, nothing else really works that well. But we're not talking about hedonic happiness—the kind of happiness that comes with epic self-indulgence in exotic locales, opulent settings, and mood enhancing stimulants. We're talking about redemptive happiness—the kind of happiness that saves you from never knowing who you could have been or what you could have achieved, both for yourself and your people.

I've never met a miserable, sad, listless, flat, or uninspired agent of resilience. Finding your source of redemptive happiness is the fuel on which you must run if you're going to help people feel safe so they can take bold risks and win. Whoever you are and whatever you do, find the time to replenish yourself at a soul level. No matter how hard your life is, find things to laugh about or celebrate. It could be massive marquee moments like a birth, a wedding, a windfall, a breakthrough, or an epiphany. Or it could be an everyday moment like a walk, a kiss, a meal, a bath, or a good night's sleep. Small things are big if you appreciate just how much you would miss them if they were gone: a perfectly baked lemon tart, a finely hit tennis ball, a glorious weekend in Hawaii, a cedar-plank salmon straight off the barbeque, an earnest conversation with a child or grandchild, a walk with your two dogs, a bike ride, or a captivating audiobook.

THE QUICK WIN

At the start of the pandemic, Diane had just taken on the role as chief neuroscience officer at Telus, a large Canadian telecommunications company. Over the next few years, to engage and support her colleagues, she shared blog posts on topics ranging from the science regarding COVID to mental health and wellness. She wrote what she remembers as her most challenging post following the death of George Floyd. "When it came to diversity, equity, and inclusion, I was fortunate to have my kids to guide me, directly but without judgement. I also had a wonderful colleague at Telus, who shared her experience as a Black woman with such grace and equanimity. Her words and stories weren't always easy to hear, but her style made people want to listen and learn. I was determined to be an ally and she consistently encouraged without shaming me when I got it wrong.

"When I wrote a post about resilience," Diane adds, "that same colleague taught me that the word resilience has sometimes been weaponized against marginalized or vulnerable groups. Some heard it as, 'Suck it up, Buttercup.' I hadn't imagined that would be the case, but once I was aware, I changed my message to include the fact that resilience should never mean accepting bullying, racism, or sexism. However, resilience can absolutely help us to weather those storms, and other life challenges, with grace and dignity, and embolden us to courageously demand better."

This "Quick Win" has two steps:

1. There are many skills that coalesce in the term resilience: managing our expectations, anticipating and accepting change, understanding and accepting what we can and can't control, and working to ensure we speak empathically to ourselves (a compassionate internal narrative). Take a moment to consider your level of resilience. Is there work to be done? Are you sharing your experiences to build the resilience of your children, friends, and co-workers? Make a personal pledge to start a new resilience-building journey.

2. Identify people whose courage and grace inspire you to demonstrate those qualities. Intentionally make every conversation with you an uplifting experience. Extract the lesson learned from your next setback and use it to spring forward. Prioritize the things that make you healthy and happy.

19

Build on Your Maturity Factor: Be Intentional

THINK OF YOUR HAPPY PLACE—the place that fills and thrills you with absolute pleasure. Think of the first time you experienced it. Think of how you absorbed your surroundings—how you were alert to every feature and nuance of your new paradise. Think of the joy you experienced and how that changed your behaviour and outlook. Think of how you related to the people around you and how you made them feel. Now think about how just thinking about it brings you pleasure.

Welcome to the science of dopamine—the pleasure (and pain) hormone that we referenced previously. Dopamine is released from a part of the brain called the nucleus accumbens, which plays a critical role in pleasure, reward, motivation, pain relief, and, unsurprisingly, addiction. The nucleus accumbens is part of the brain's reward circuit motivating us to seek pleasure and avoid pain, both of which are critical for survival. It stores information about the associated environmental stimuli, enabling us to repeat pleasurable experiences and avoid the aversive ones. The pleasurable high of an addictive substance is provoked by the release of dopamine in the nucleus accumbens that also strongly pairs that pleasure with other stimuli, which fosters compulsive drug seeking after exposure to a related environmental cue (e.g., a smoker craving a cigarette in particular environments or when they smell cigarette smoke).

Knowing what gives you pleasure and the consequences of pursuing it, together with knowing what causes you pain and the consequences of avoiding it, are important cornerstones of maturity. Maturity is the essence of good judgement. It's the capacity to understand the impact of your actions in advance. It's impossible to build a safe space around you without the forward thinking and critical thinking that come with brain maturation. The pursuit of pleasure or the avoidance of pain without regard to potential negative consequences can cause great harm to relationships, businesses, and society. Inner character means recognizing and managing our urges before they cause harm. Effective leadership is about investing people with a sense of safety and confidence by consistently demonstrating that capacity to them. Unfortunately, it can take one rash act to infuse them with doubt about your next move, your motivation, or your sincerity.

Your level of maturity governs your response to extreme circumstances. When you're highly aroused or upset, you're not able to use all of the skills that come with maturity. That's when you need to pause, reflect, and confer with trusted confidantes or advisors.

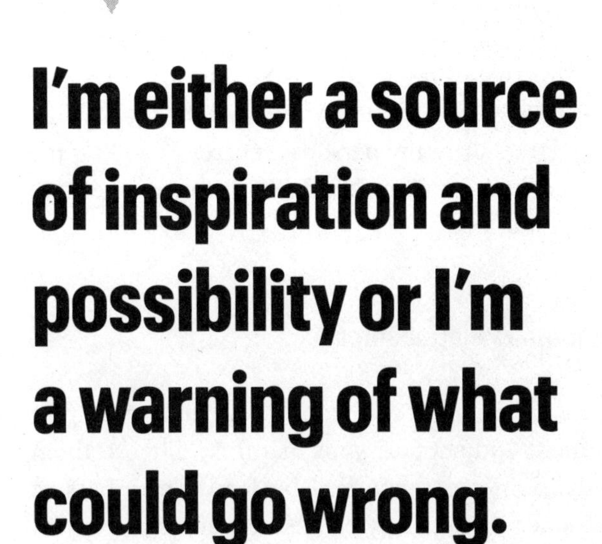

I'm either a source of inspiration and possibility or I'm a warning of what could go wrong.

In such circumstances, Diane refers to her need to call on her own senate. Canada's first prime minister, Sir John A. Macdonald, famously called the Senate a chamber of sober second thought. "Sometimes, I need to be my own senate," Diane shares. "I need to take the time to slow my brain down and carefully reflect on a crisis situation with less emotion. If I can't sort it out myself, I turn to my own professional senate—one or two of my most trusted advisors—to walk through the challenge and the possible solutions. My husband and children sit in my personal senate, providing me with a sober second thought when I need it (and sometimes when I don't think I do!)."

Build Intentional Relationships

The people with whom you surround yourself will impact your judgement and support your maturity. Choose them intentionally. Some of them may be family members or long-time friends. Others may be business associates or colleagues. They can even be specialist professionals that you pay to provide you with the required insights or information. Eventually, we all become the calibre of the company we keep. And just as we want others to be there for us when we need them, we need to be there for them.

The worldwide pandemic has stretched many relationships to breaking points. It impacted how we live, love, and work. Now we're experiencing the never-ending repercussions on our families, finances, and sense of security. None of us feel as safe as we used to. We gravitate toward people who can boost our sense of safety and help us navigate the future—in short, those who make us feel like we belong.

Some of us, by nature, mature earlier than others. They're the people we think of as "old souls." They've always been the adults in the room—even as kids. They're the genetically gifted ones. We all come out of the womb with our temperament baked in, but they just happen to have a built-in balance. The rest of us have to work hard at building our maturity.

Personally, I can track the defining crises of my life to my inherent lack of maturity. In my moments of elevated emotions, I didn't consider how the next action would impact my life. Whether it was the investments I made, the relationships I squandered, or the lifestyle I maintained, it all came down to the inability to ask or answer this question: How will this decision impact my life?

Now the first question I consciously ask myself is: How will this decision impact my life and the lives of the people I care about? I'm acutely aware that every decision I make makes it easier or harder for others to support me. If I'm irresponsible, impetuous, or self-indulgent, I not only prejudice my own interests, I jeopardize others' support of me. I'm either a source of inspiration and possibility, or I'm a warning of what could go wrong. I never want people to second-guess themselves when it comes to either helping me or accepting my help.

THE QUICK WIN

Think of how you're consciously avoiding situations or activities that could harm or upset others. Think of situations or activities that bring you pleasure and benefit others. Resolve to always ask yourself this question: How will this decision impact my life and the lives of the people I care about?

1. Focus On Achieving the Best Outcome
2. Map Out the Steps Required to Reach Your Destination
3. Build Your Team
4. Celebrate Your Wins—Size Doesn't Count
5. Confront Your Negative Thoughts
6. Prepare for the Breakdown
7. Keep the Faith

7 STEPS TO BUILDING THE FUTURE

PROCRASTINATION IS THE act of intentionally and unnecessarily putting off a task that should be completed. That task is often, but not always, associated with pain, difficulty, or discomfort. It could be just plain boring, but it still needs to be done. A high level of procrastination is usually inversely correlated to maturity.

If you know you should do something, but you don't want to do it, you're putting your future at risk. The more important the task that you're putting off, the greater the consequences not just to you but to all the people who will be impacted by it. The more you procrastinate, the more habitual it becomes. Every time you procrastinate, you contract while the task expands.

Always the psychiatrist, Diane reminds me that procrastination is associated with some psychiatric disorders, particularly attention deficit hyperactivity disorder (ADHD). People who have ADHD struggle to focus on things they don't find interesting, like math, but can hyper-focus on activities that engage them, like video games. "Before you think, 'How is that different from every other kid in the world?' know that ADHD is one of the most inheritable psychiatric disorders, with a similar genetic risk to bipolar disorder," Diane says. "It's not like people with ADHD don't try to focus. They can't. And it's so frustrating, humiliating, and disheartening for them. Their distractibility, disorganization, procrastination, and inability to focus don't have anything to do with intelligence. The areas of the brain that are responsible for those activities aren't wired the same way as people who don't have ADHD. If procrastination is related to ADHD or another psychiatric disorder that is affecting your cognitive functioning, like depression or severe anxiety, it's important to seek professional help."

If, however, procrastination is a proxy for lack of maturity, how can you prevail over it? Recognition is the first critical step. People often don't recognize the burden of their chronic procrastination until they're facing a deadline they can't possibly meet. Once it's past and the repercussions are realized, whether through reprimand, failure, or job loss, they might go back to the same old patterns.

If you see yourself in this description, it's time to make a change, but take small bites. Keep a list of "must dos," set an alarm for each one, *never* turn off the alarm until a firm plan is made to tackle it (and then set a new alarm), and celebrate every win—each strike-through or check is rewiring your brain to procrastinate less. Consciously focus on the joy, relief, or fulfillment that comes from getting the job done. These small actions will literally drive the release of dopamine in your nucleus accumbens, your brain's pleasure center, and will also diminish the pain of failing to meet a critical deadline or letting someone you care about down. Self-stimulating dopamine is the ultimate fuel of success.

Trust me when I tell you that writing this book stretched me to my max. Every day was a duel between the desire to run away from the rigour required to write it and the feeling of accomplishment arising from actually getting the words out and on the screen. I'm not a chronic procrastinator—I pay my bills on time, make the calls I dread, and take the garbage out the night before. But for momentous tasks that require a Herculean effort, sometimes it takes a village. As a team, Diane and I followed these steps to maintain momentum on our major project, this book, and triumph over more than procrastination. We needed to find the time, in a sea of competing priorities, to make this dream a reality. As you walk through the following steps with me, think of the thing that you're delaying because it's causing you anxiety and how you can take it on *now*:

1. Focus On Achieving the Best Outcome

Find reasons to believe you can achieve your goals. Experience the delight and satisfaction of your successes in advance. See them. Feel them. Hear them. Taste them. Smell them. In my case, I could see the book. I could feel the pride and kudos that come with its publication. I could hear the accolades and applause of my audiences. I could taste the champagne of celebration. I could smell the pages and ink. What's it for you?

2. Map Out the Steps Required to Reach Your Destination

Identify the first step, then the second, then the third. If you can't see the fourth and fifth steps, trust that they will appear after you take the third step. In my case, I conceptualized the book. Then I approached Diane. Then I approached my publisher, Page Two. Then I set up weekly conversations with Diane. Then I transcribed each conversation and turned it into a chapter. Then I worked with James Harbeck, our editor; Cameron McKague, our designer;

Indu Singh, our copy editor; and Diane to tighten the text and turn it into a compelling storyline. And voila, eighteen months later, the first copy of *You Belong Here* rolled off the presses. What are your first three steps?

3. Build Your Team

Select the people who will push or pull you into your desired future state. Be clear on your expectations of them. Invite them to hold you accountable. Own your commitment to them. In my case, I owned my commitment to a litany of people: Diane; Page Two; my business partner, Michael Adams, CEO of the Environics group of companies; my wife, Hilary, who pushed me forward every step of the way; my future clients who needed to hear this content; my readers who wanted to read this content; my social network who let me know they expected this content; and perhaps most importantly, to myself. I need to have my whole heart in a project like this, to make it all it can be. Who are your team members?

4. Celebrate Your Wins—Size Doesn't Count

Every time you conceptualize the win, you take a hit of dopamine. It could be a tiny step forward, a reassuring signal, an acknowledgement from a key stakeholder, or simply a determination to keep on keeping on. Seek feedback—any feedback is a win because it shows others' engagement in your endeavour. Reward yourself with treats along the way. The bigger the breakthrough, the bigger the treat. In my case, every sentence was a win. Every conversation with Diane was a treat. Every enhancement from James Harbeck was a leap forward. My treats ranged from a single malt scotch at the end of a writing session to a trip to France at the conclusion of the first draft. What wins can you celebrate?

Even when you receive criticism, consciously receive it as a gift. Esther Bintliff, writing in the *Financial Times* (July 24, 2022), suggests that we go through three stages when we receive criticism: The first, with apologies for the language, is "Fuck you." The second is "I suck." And the third is "Let's make it better." As an agent of belonging, your job is to get to stage three as rapidly as possible, helping others accelerate their transformation as well. The alternative can be damaging. Bintliff quotes extensive research that shows that in 38 percent of cases, feedback not only did not improve performance, it actively made it worse. Even positive feedback can backfire. Much of how we respond to feedback is driven by the nature of our relationship with the person giving it. If you feel loved and cared for by the provider, you're more likely to accept, process, and act on their feedback.

5. Confront Your Negative Thoughts

Don't succumb to your fear. Don't use euphemisms that take the sting out of your inaction. At the same time, treat yourself with compassion. Be alert to the regret you will feel the moment after you neglect your mission. Remind yourself to maintain your step-wise approach—each step is the one that empowers you to take the next. It's difficult, but that's how you build your muscle. Honour the person that looks at you in the mirror every day. Confront your automatic negative thoughts with that perspective and create thoughts that change the way you approach a challenge—one bite at a time.

Writing this book gives Diane and me immense pleasure because it's so many activities rolled into one: social interaction, explaining people's behaviour through science, creating new ideas, helping people, receiving encouraging feedback, and fulfilling our personal purposes.

Diane's dopamine hit is "How do I change the world for people who are living with mental illness?" She believes she can have a meaningful impact on that vulnerable population. She has had family members who suffered from mental illness and, of course, she has treated thousands of patients. She also wants to be present for her children and ensure the well-being of her family. There are lots of Dianes, and they are all integrated. What makes her a good mom and partner is also what makes her a good friend and professional leader. Life may not be fair, but she can try to make it more fair for those that have been dealt an unfair hand.

My dopamine hit is to activate people into doing something, because something always comes from something. Nothing comes from nothing. I want to free people from the torture of regret. It's better to do something imperfectly than not do it at all.

What's your dopamine hit?

6. Prepare for the Breakdown

Dopamine depletion is inevitable, especially when the task is Herculean. There will be times when you feel like there are no wins to celebrate. You'll find yourself in a dark place, but in a dark place is also where you'll find yourself. That's when you need to replenish your dopamine reservoir. It can be done through physical activity that increases the BDNF (brain-derived neurotropic factor) we discussed earlier. It's your brain cell fertilizer that treats and prevents depression and anxiety. Social interaction and support from friends, family, and close colleagues will also revitalize you. Talk therapy can also shift the way you view your challenges—hearing yourself speak and getting feedback from a skilled guide can make a remarkable difference. Getting out there and helping others can also have a big impact—even just reaching out to someone who would benefit from talking to you.

As a coach, I have a coach with whom I speak weekly. She doesn't give me solutions. She only asks me questions so that I discover the answers for myself. Here are some of them:

- Can you see yourself delivering the results you just said you wanted?
- Is your present activity a match for the desired future you want to create?
- Will you be committed to following through?
- What could you create as a possibility that will empower you?
- What actions are required to make your goal a reality?
- What would it look like to succeed beyond your wildest dreams?
- Do you have what you need to deal with the specific challenge in front of you right now?
- How can you use what you have?

7. Keep the Faith

The science tells us that people with a systematized belief are better able to master their difficulties. Faith, either religious or secular, provides you with the conviction and peace of mind that you will succeed. If you absolutely know that you (and your higher power) will find a way, it becomes a self-fulfilling prophecy.

Diane's faith is expressed in a simple credo: I will conduct myself to the benefit of others. So when she treats a patient, she asks herself: Am I treating this patient the way I would want my child to be treated? When she leads her team, she asks herself: Am I creating a compassionate culture where people feel safe to take risks? When she interacts with me, she's always asking: Am I giving you what you need? For Diane, conducting herself to the benefit of others is her definition of integrity. When she's operating with integrity, she's unstoppable. When she isn't, she's immediately and deeply uncomfortable. She'll change course or change the people with whom she's working.

My credo is: I'm inspired to inspire. I will do whatever it takes to excite people into actions they otherwise wouldn't have taken. My definition of integrity is being a model of the desired behaviour. I must be congruent. I do what I say and I say what I do. Any disconnect weakens and unsettles me. I'll keep going until the job is done. Then I'll take on a new one.

What's your credo?

20

Ask Where You Are Going Next

DIANE AND I have learned that business is a bunch of people coming together and pretending they know what's going to happen in the next five to ten years.

Yes, it's impossible to know, but organizations continue to push their team members to prepare for unknown unknowns. They need the confidence, even if it's delusional, to move forward. They must have the grit to go through the sheer grind of confronting the impossible every day. They must also build excitement around concepts that people believe will enrich their lives or boost their capacity to succeed.

Yes, there are broad trends that provide a rough guide to the long term—demographics, lifestyle, geography, technology, politics, medicine, quest for efficiency, and speed. But within those parameters, anything and everything can and will happen. Whether it's a deadly pandemic, a brutal war, or an errant economy, the future makes fools of us all.

No one is clairvoyant. Visionaries don't see the future, they create it, turning the proverb "necessity is the mother of invention" on its head. Steve Jobs showed, through the iPhone and Apple Music, that invention is the mother of necessity—no one needed to have immediate access to every song ever recorded, much less an iPhone, until they could. Mark Zuckerberg, Sergey Brin, Larry Page, Walt Disney, Oprah Winfrey, and other great innovators did the same in their respective fields.

In the end, all success comes down to human beings doing their best. They're making up stories, rationalizing outcomes, recovering from mistakes, and creating their own realities. We're all relying on other people to craft a story we can believe in—supported by the facts. We need to think in chunks of time that are reasonable while we prepare ourselves for other contingencies that will almost always shock and surprise us. We call this activity "planning."

Plans will always be flawed. As the Navy SEALs say, "No plan survives first contact with the enemy." It's not the plan that achieves the win; it's the willingness to plan, then change the plan, then change it again and again and again. Plan works best as a verb. As a noun, it's obsolete the moment it's complete. Planning focuses the mind on finding solutions that the plan is designed to solve. It's a source of confidence and self-empowerment that transfers itself to others. People are attracted to people who appear to know where they're going. Especially in times of extreme change, the belief that you have a plan can be interpreted by others as "It's safe to take risks in pursuit of big goals."

Have you ever been so good that you amazed yourself? It may have been a presentation that you delivered, a deal that you closed, a project that you nailed, a crisis that you resolved, a team that you inspired, a person that you coached, or blog you posted. The golden thread through every outcome was your ability to exceed your own expectations and achieve more than you imagined possible. Take a look at those moments and ask yourself what enabled you to perform at that level. The answer will be that you kept your end in mind and followed the steps required to achieve it. The end-in-mind and steps may have come to you as an epiphany or as a carefully controlled campaign, but they invested your activity with power and effectiveness. They blinkered you against doubt and distraction. They made you believe in you. Now your mission must be to make them a habit.

1. Declare Your Purpose
2. Declare Your Goals
3. Declare Your Strategy

THE 3 FUNDAMENTALS OF PLANNING

IF ANTICIPATION IS the act of looking forward, planning is the system of disciplined anticipation that sharpens your vision and drives your capacity to achieve it. It is simple but it isn't easy. If you're willing to implement these three fundamentals of planning, you'll brand yourself as someone who creates belonging and is a Keeper of the Safety Flame—someone who realizes their own dreams while helping others realize theirs. We'll show you how we used them to create this book. In turn, we invite you to create your three fundamentals of planning as you go through this exercise with us. Get a fresh notebook where you can write down all your thoughts.

1. Declare Your Purpose

Your purpose is your why. It's the reason you're doing something. At a basic level, your purpose in going to the store could be to buy milk, bread, butter, and eggs for breakfast. The importance you place on that purpose motivates action: your family needs that food and you love to cook for them. At a higher level, your purpose must inspire you every day and should be imbued with urgency, enthusiasm, and love. Some call it their North Star. A deeper purpose can be personal, professional, or shared with a team. Every day, Diane hopes her team starts work energized because they've agreed upon a shared purpose: to change the world for people living with mental illness.

Why do you work every day? Is it just like going to the store, or does it bring something more to your life? Do you feel a gravitational pull toward something bigger or deeper? What do you love to do? What do you believe you could be great at doing? Where can you make the biggest contribution to your world? What would enable you to get the highest return on your life investment of time, energy, or treasure, so that when you come to the end of it, you can say, I gave it my all?

You'll notice we said *declare* your purpose, not just *define* it. Declare means to make known in an emphatic manner. It means publicly announcing your purpose, making others aware and inspiring them at the same time. You can begin by sending your declaration to me at mike.lipkin@environics.ca.

When you declare something important to yourself and to others, you start building their belief in you. You invite them to trust you. You set yourself up for success if you're totally committed to following through. You enable others to understand your why, and you open up their minds and hearts to believing in your message. You co-create credibility with them in advance of your deliverables. Yes, there is risk—you're raising expectations. But the alternative is irrelevance. If others don't know your raison d'être, and if it doesn't inspire them, you'll mean a lot less to them. Even worse, they might make one up for you that misrepresents who you are.

2. Declare Your Goals

Your goals are the ends toward which your effort is directed. Like a soccer or hockey player, they are the net into which you're aiming your ball or puck. They should stir your blood and stretch you to your max. When you think of them, you should be scared and excited in equal measure. There is nothing about this book that isn't either scary or exciting. Sometimes, the only difference between the two is the mood we're in.

We have created the DART model of goal-setting:

- Definite—it must be clear and explicit.
- Audacious—it must be bold, daring, disruptive, and practical.
- Resolute—it must withstand doubt and setbacks.
- Time-bound—it must have a date by which the goal will be achieved.

Diane and I believe in setting twelve-to-twenty-four-month goals because the future is too unpredictable to think too far past that. Even as we've created this book together, we've adjusted what we've had to deliver on a rolling month-by-month basis. We're always looking ahead, but not too far ahead. We can always see the finish line from where we stand—even if it moves along the way. We're audacious but still practical. That's how we protect ourselves against overwhelm or loss of direction.

Send me your DART goals. I'm at mike.lipkin@environics.ca.

Being timid won't keep you safe. It will just condemn you to regret later on.

3. Declare Your Strategy

Your strategy is a disciplined method for consistently achieving your desired results. It's the ingredients and formula that enable your success. It's part art and part science. Here is our strategy for creating and marketing this book:

1. **Scan for the need.** Diane and I live in the world of treating mental illness and growing mental health. We study and understand the trends, the pitfalls, the science, the politics, the service providers, the technology, and the economics of the field. We identified the opportunity to combine our talents to satisfy what we believe to be a crucial need: creating a safe space of belonging that empowers people to take risks. We wanted to go beyond just facilitating psychological safety to fostering high-performance safety.

2. **Play to our strengths.** Together, Diane and I are a formidable team. We complement each other perfectly. We have the same goals and purpose, but very different skill sets. She brings the science, and I bring the art of marketing, motivation, and sales. Our combined offering is unprecedented. Based on our research, we believe there is nothing else like it.

3. **Create a powerful value proposition.** Every great strategy balances on a powerful value proposition that can be explained in a statement. Our value prop is: *You Belong Here* will help make people feel safe to take risks that help them win. The win represents fulfillment on every level: mental, emotional, social, and financial.

4. **Design, produce, and package a phenomenal product or service.** While Diane and I created the raw content for this book, it needed another level of skill to refine,

edit, and polish it. We hired the wizards at Page Two publishing to do that for us. Both Diane and I have published books through Page Two before, so we knew their genius. Page Two also consulted with us on the financial considerations of production costs, book pricing, royalties, and other publishing esoterica.

5. **Distribute, market, and sell through every appropriate channel.** We've identified Amazon as our primary medium for selling the analog version of the book, Kindle for selling the ebook version, iTunes and Audible for selling the audio version. We will also sell direct to organizations as part of our workshop strategy. We will publicize *You Belong Here* through our personal networks, podcasts, and the traditional media with whom we have cultivated long-term relationships. We will also encourage every reader or listener to become a mobilizer on our behalf. So, if you feel like this book has made a difference to you, please review it on Amazon, tell a friend or, better yet, buy them a copy.

THE QUICK WIN

Craft your strategy. Share it with me and other important people in your network. Begin now. Your future will grow from the seeds you plant today, and I mean literally *today*.

21

Know That the Ultimate Safety Zone Is Courageous Creativity

"WHAT LIES behind you and what lies in front of you pales in comparison to what lies inside of you," said Ralph Waldo Emerson. If you know you have everything you need to achieve everything you want, you can live a life of fulfillment and freedom from fear. But having everything you need doesn't mean you have all the ready-made resources or tools you need on demand. It means that you can make them up as you go along. You can imagine and implement them into existence as you need them. You have the courage to experiment with the confidence that you will succeed. The safety zone is not a comfort zone. It's better.

Throughout this book, what we have shared are ways in which you can create a safety zone for yourself and others. But a safety zone is not a walled garden, keeping you in. You are not truly safe if you can't be all that you could be. The ultimate safety zone is one you bring with you and create as you move forward. It's knowing that you have the creativity to handle any challenge that comes at you. And when you create this ultimate safety zone for yourself, you help create it for others, too.

We define *courageous creativity* very simply: it's the recognized ability to access your inner and outer resources to achieve your goals and find optimal solutions to your challenges—whatever they are. If you own this definition of courageous creativity, you'll never feel stuck or blocked. You'll find your path or build a new path. You'll retain your optimism and passion for the grind, no matter how intense it becomes. Edwin Land, the co-founder of Polaroid corporation and the inventor of the Polaroid instant camera, expressed this notion best: "Any problem can be solved with the materials available in the room at the time."

In 2022, the verb "MacGyver" was added to the *Merriam-Webster Online Dictionary*. As *Merriam-Webster* states, "Angus MacGyver, as portrayed by actor Richard Dean Anderson in the titular, action-packed television series *MacGyver*, was many things—including a secret agent, a Swiss Army knife enthusiast, and a convert to vegetarianism... In fact, so memorable was this man... and his ability to use whatever was available to him—often simple things, such as a paper clip, chewing gum, or a rubber band—to escape a sticky situation or to make a device to help him complete a mission, that people began associating his name with making quick fixes or finding innovative solutions to immediate problems. Hence the verb *MacGyver*, a slang term meaning to 'make, form, or repair (something) with what is conveniently on hand.'"

MacGyver epitomizes the essence of what we've defined as courageous creativity. There is always something or someone around you that you can call upon to achieve a breakthrough.

What would you take on if you had no room to fail? What do you care so much about that you're willing to take on your bogeymen and nemeses? What are your natural gifts that you can honour by using them? Who are the people standing by to guide and support you forward? How can you set up your support infrastructure to sustain your progress? What are you waiting for?

I would love to hear about how you're chasing your moonshot. Write me at mike.lipkin@environics.ca. On the other hand, I know there are many reasons why you may not be pursuing your dream. You've been too busy just surviving. You've never seriously considered it. You've resigned yourself to a life that's good, not great. You just haven't discovered a goal that fires you up, triggers a dopamine surge and gets your neurons firing and rewiring. You don't see yourself as a creative person who can excite others into action.

It's time to take a stand on behalf of yourself and all the people you can help to achieve their dreams. Take inventory of your gifts—internal and external. Record all the times you've accessed your inner and outer resources to achieve your goals and find optimal solutions to life's inevitable challenges. Remember what it felt like to surprise yourself and delight others. Think and act like that kind of person. Activate your appetite for more. Tell other people what you're up to. Dare to risk and risk by daring. Invite breakthroughs into your life by showing that you mean it. Being timid won't keep you safe. It will just condemn you to regret later on.

Commit to the Vision That You Have of Yourself

By our definition of courageous creativity, you need to have a strong conviction that you are creative. Otherwise, you'll be defeated by the obstacles you encounter. The greater the reward, the greater the courage that is required to achieve it. If you achieve a position of prominence, you should expect to be attacked or criticized often. Your stated opinions may even be weaponized against you. It comes with the territory. It may always hurt, because skin that is too thick can also make you numb and insensitive, but pain should never be a reason not to chase your dream.

We're all human brands whose every action builds or diminishes our equity with others. Our vision for ourselves must also be a vision that empowers others to chase their dreams. We've learned that people who live extraordinary lives are ambitious enough to believe they can achieve their goals. They don't just adapt to the world. They also make the world adapt to them. In other words, they don't just follow the rules. They make up rules for others to follow. Every innovation breaks an existing rule of how something should be done and sets up a new one. Innovation is the mother of necessity.

A glittering example is how Deloris Jordan, Michael Jordan's mother, negotiated a royalty agreement with Nike in the launch of Air Jordan, rather than just a flat endorsement fee. This led to almost two billion dollars in lifetime earnings for Michael, and a new standard for endorsement deals with athletes from that point on! Great entrepreneurs of every colour, creed, or community reset the rules of the game. And they create a new and expanded safety zone of creativity for others.

The best yardstick is the judgement of people who love and understand you.

• • • • •

The Own-Your-Brain Test

All her years as a psychiatrist have taught Diane that the time to act is when "our brain is our own." In other words, we need to make decisions when our cognitive capacity is intact. We need to be careful that we don't create internal hurricanes that destroy our internal neighbourhoods. When you're depressed, anxious, enraged, or completely overwhelmed, you're not cognizant of what's right for you. You're acting with a diminished decision-making capacity. You're guaranteeing yourself future heartbreak when you look back at the poor judgement you will have displayed. After years of experience, Diane has learned to speak openly to her patients about making potentially life altering decisions. "If you're struggling through a serious mental illness, postpone crucial decisions if you possibly can. Deciding to move across the country, quit your job, or leave your partner when you're cognitively impaired too often leads to regret, because your executive brain isn't able to fully engage. Worse, you might not be aware of how impaired your cognition is, while those who care about you fret on the sidelines as you push ahead. Recover. Reflect. Review. Re-engage. Get the love, compassion, and perspective of people who can replenish your sense of potency. When you feel like you're at your best again, whether it takes an hour, a day, a week, or a year, then you should decide and take action."

The best yardstick of whether you're at your best is the judgement of people who love and understand you. They are also the ones who are most able to appreciate and comprehend your situation. They are open and candid with you. They are a combination of professional and personal associates. They could be your doctor, lawyer, accountant, colleague, boss, client, spouse, or friend. You need to be open to their feedback no matter how hard it may be to accept. That's why a good coach or therapist is valuable—their guidance is literally clinical. When you're in a weakened state, you often don't realize how impaired your decision-making capacity has become. This is why people deny the severity of their deficits—especially men who are resistant to confessing their helplessness. In response to the question, "What the heck were you thinking?" Too often, the answer is, "I have no idea."

The time to maximize your courageous creativity is when it's the last thing you feel like doing. That's when your energy is at its lowest and you're tempted to give it all up. Disappointment and frustration can shrivel your resourcefulness, but those are the moments when you need to recapture your mojo and reignite your passion. Working toward a transformative goal isn't always sunshine and rainbows. In fact, it probably sucks a lot of the time, but when things are at their worst, we need to believe they can only get better. That belief enables us to refocus on being our best. The more we practice this discipline, the better we become. The own-your-brain test will help you determine whether you're moving in the right direction.

Schedule quarterly check-ins with your key stakeholders. Ask them questions like:

- How do you think I'm doing?
- Are you happy with my performance and contribution?
- These are the areas I'm working on. Where do you think I can improve?
- What areas do you think I should be focusing on?
- Do you think I'm helping others grow and develop? Or do you think I'm cramping others' style?

Every Story Has a Beginning, a Middle, and an End

Just before he died of pancreatic cancer on October 5, 2011, Steve Jobs said, "Remembering that I'll be dead soon is the most important tool I've ever encountered to help me make the big choices in life." He knew his time was almost up, so he endeavoured to make the most of the time he had left. Those who are fortunate enough to have clean bills of health often suffer from a complacency that lulls them into inertia. The truth is that nobody knows how much time they have left. None of us has been promised a precise supply of tomorrows.

Growing your courageous creativity is a function of reflection and urgency in equal measure. Reading this book has probably been a time of reflection for you. We hope you've found ways to review and reimagine your narrative. It's time to write your next chapter. Begin with this exercise that will galvanize you into action: Think of who you want to be in three years' time. Imagine yourself, three years from now, living your best life possible. What will you be doing? What will you be celebrating? Now look at the you-of-today: Are you setting up the you-of-three-years'-time for the success you deserve? Don't make the you-of-three-years'-time angry with the you-of-today because you didn't do everything you could with everything you have when you had the opportunities to do so.

THE QUICK WIN

Diane shares, "Like many young people, especially young women, I had wicked imposter syndrome. I was so sure my dream of becoming a doctor would never happen, so I never told anyone I wanted to be a doctor. I didn't tell anyone I applied to pharmacy school until I was accepted. I didn't tell anyone I applied for medical school until I was accepted (except my future husband, because he had to drive me to my MCAT). It wasn't until the day of my medical school graduation that I finally had to accept that I was worthy of my place in that class. Until then, I saw every success as a fluke. I was sure I'd be caught and exposed as a fraud because I really didn't belong. Coming first in my medical school class, which was completely astonishing and unexpected, sucker-punched my inner imposter. I wish I could say she was down for the count. The wind was definitely taken out of her sails, but my inner imposter still got up and punched me back, now and again.

"For a big part of my life, I never felt like I belonged anywhere. A chaotic childhood, countless schools and moves, and a lack of consistent parenting set me up to struggle to become an adult. I didn't appreciate almost anything about myself. I've now learned that I'm responsible for creating the life I want to lead. I need to surround myself with wonderful people. I need to create a workplace where I want to work. I need to treat people like I want to be treated. I need to foster a sense of belonging in every relationship I value. Every person I invest in gives me back so much more. That's what makes the times I've screwed up and invested in the wrong person—the rare psychopaths I've encountered—matter so little. My life, personally and professionally, is rich beyond measure. I didn't deserve my life. I worked damn hard for it and I'm proud of what I've achieved."

Recall a recent time when you demonstrated courageous creativity—the recognized ability to access your inner and outer resources to achieve your goals and solve your problems, whatever they are. In the next week, practice courageous creativity by MacGyvering a solution with whatever is conveniently on hand. Express the vision you have of yourself and share it with key stakeholders—then live it. Set the you-of-three-years'-time up for success by doing something remarkable in the next week.

And seize every opportunity to foster others' creativity. Help them MacGyver their way forward. Encourage them to express their vision and share it. Help ensure that the them-of-three-years'-time are successful because of what you helped them do today.

EPILOGUE

Become the Safe-Haven-Recharging-Station

According to the Society for Human Resource Management (SHRM), maintaining employee morale and engagement is the number one priority of HR leaders in North America today. At the same time, according to Gallup, a leading human capital firm, only 32 percent of full- and part-time employees working for organizations are engaged, while 18 percent are actively disengaged.

Gallup research also shows that disengaged employees have a 37 percent higher absenteeism rate. This results in 18 percent lower productivity and 15 percent lower profitability. Disengaged employees also have a direct negative impact on the customer experience and client satisfaction, leading to even further costs in the long run.

Making people feel like they belong so they feel really safe to be their best, take bold risks, and win is the antidote to disengagement. It's also a powerful way to enhance their quality of life beyond the workplace. People who feel like they're members of winning teams carry that winning spirit wherever they go. According to Fred Reichheld, creator of the Net Promoter Score and the author of *Winning on Purpose*, "80 percent of the variation in team member happiness could be explained by how much team members agreed with a single statement: I feel like a valued member of a team that wins with its customers."

Our well-being is a direct function of our sense of belonging to wherever we are at that moment. I can track my personal well-being to the acute moments of belonging that I have experienced over the past twenty-two years. I felt a sense of belonging when I moved to Toronto from my native Johannesburg, South Africa, in 2001. I felt a sense of belonging when I formed a joint venture with Michael Adams and the remarkable team at Environics Research Group in 2002. I felt a sense of belonging when I discovered the extraordinary Landmark Education community in 2006 that has informed and inspired me to be my best. I felt a sense of belonging when I contracted with the Leadership Circle Profile (LCP) in 2017 to become an LCP coach.

I feel a sense of belonging every time I connect with a client or partner that shares my values and aspires to making a difference, including my co-author, Diane. And, of course, I feel a sense of belonging every time I wake up next to my fabulous wife, Hilary. I belong wherever she is.

Throughout this book, we've given you tools to foster a sense of belonging in whomever you meet. We've also invited you to create your own ways of connecting with others. Now it's time to put the tools into practice. Reach out and make as many people as possible feel really safe to take big risks and win with you.

To paraphrase Bob Dylan, be the shelter in the storm. In a world of accelerating volatility, become the safe-haven-recharging-station that magnetizes the best and the brightest to you.

That's all, folks! Please let us know the difference that this book has made to you and the differences that you are making for others. Write us at mike.lipkin@environics.ca. Until then, thank you for staying with me until the final word. Here's to spreading a sense of belonging wherever we go!

Acknowledgements

Mike Lipkin

It's a miraculous moment for me to look back on the production of *You Belong Here* and contemplate the myriad people that helped make it possible.

I want to begin by acknowledging Canada, my adopted home and native land. Canadians' openness to my brand of motivation and communication has liberated me to play at my best for the past twenty-three years since I landed here in 2001.

I want to thank my wife, Hilary, for giving me her unequivocal support and encouragement to swing for the moon. There were many times during the writing of this book that she shook me out of my procrastination to get back to my desk and just write.

I want to thank Diane McIntosh, a gift from my Higher Power. From the very first time I met her, I knew she was a special person with a huge heart and an even bigger brain. When I first mentioned the possibility of writing a book with her, in 2018, it was a pipe dream. Now it's a reality. *You Belong Here* would have been literally impossible without her.

I want to thank all my long-standing clients that continue to challenge, stretch, and believe in me. Dave O'Neil, Lorenzo Santini, Susan Uthayakumar, Mike Parra, Lee Cooper, Silvio Stroescu, Kim Yost, Mike Laranjo, Allison Rosenthal, John Ruffolo, Mark Maybank, Jeff Marchand, Bettina Hamelin, Jeff Dufour, Karen Azlen, and Erez Pikar, to name just a few.

I want to thank my business partners—Michael Adams for his continuous inspiration and guidance, Christian Roy for his counsel and ongoing generation of opportunities, Heather Pirzas for her extraordinary translation of my work into killer presentations, Lowell Brown for digitally empowering me, Liv Tyler for her passionate execution of the ideas I throw at her, and Brian Blosser for keeping the financials on track.

I want to thank the entire team at Page Two for producing a third masterpiece for me. From the first conversation to the actual printing of the book, they were spectacular. Jesse Finkelstein knows exactly how to say the right words to keep nudging us forward. Adrineh Der-Boghossian and Ashley Rayner project-managed Diane and me to perfection. James Harbeck configured and reconfigured the narrative until it told the truth. Indu Singh edited the manuscript and made it pristine. Cameron McKague created another visual delight.

Finally, I want to thank medical science, my personal psychiatrist, Gayle Gordon, and my personal doctor, Marla Shapiro, for helping to extend my longevity. I never thought I would make it this far, never mind doing my best work over the next twenty years.

Dr. Diane McIntosh

The opportunity to write this book came at the worst possible time for me. I was in the midst of launching a new medical technology, RAPIDS, that entailed building a team, negotiating all the twists and turns of a start-up, and trying to maintain a healthy work-life balance. Mike's ability to keep me on task, all the while respecting my other time commitments and never once making me feel guilty, speaks volumes. He wanted us to work together to create something truly valuable, and to do so, he made me feel appreciated and respected. He also made our weekly conversations lively, provocative, and entertaining. The joy of the journey has made the fruits of our labour even sweeter. Thank you, Mike, for being an incredible (non-psychopathic) partner in crime.

My deepest gratitude, now and always, to my husband, Stuart, and our two children, Robert and Shannon, for giving me a rock-solid foundation, built on love, respect, and *Simpsons/Seinfeld* trivia.

Leading the development of RAPIDS informed so much of *You Belong Here* that I would be remiss if I didn't share my deep gratitude to three people who believed in me and my vision for RAPIDS. Without Darren Entwistle and Doug French, Telus' CEO and CFO, respectively, there would be no RAPIDS. The unwavering support of my partner on so many professional endeavours, Charbel Bouezz, including RAPIDS, SwitchRx, PsychedUp CME, and my book *This Is Depression*, has underpinned so much of our shared success. Charbel, you are the personification of resilience and you always, always have my back. For that, I will always be grateful.

I also want to acknowledge my incredible RAPIDS team, who have embraced our compassionate culture and work to nurture it every day. Their brilliance, drive, kindness, and grit have supported me to build RAPIDS, write this book with Mike, and maintain my sanity. Thank you, Alex, Darcy,

Nathalie, Shawn, Anoop, Lori, Mehroon, Emma, Carole, Marc, Debbie, Rob, Chris, Andrea, Oscar, Brad × 2, Katharine, Leslie, Angele, Miguel, Katie, Traycho, Roee, Souad, and Ali Y.

Finally, my heartfelt gratitude to the entire Page Two team for producing my first, and now my second, book. Jesse Finkelstein captains an engaged, thoughtful, professional team, including Adrineh Der-Boghossian, Ashley Rayner, James Harbeck, and Cameron McKague, that I trusted to guide, critique, and shepherd us to deliver this book, which has been both gratifying and a privilege to produce.

Notes

Note: The majority of the quotes attributed to Diane in this book were gathered from conversations that took place between Dr. Diane McIntosh and Mike Lipkin from June 2022 to July 2023.

Introduction

1 *they comprise about 12 percent of corporate leadership*: Simon Croom, "12% of Corporate Leaders Are Psychopaths. It's Time to Take This Problem Seriously," *Fortune*, June 6, 2021, fortune.com/2021/06/06/corporate-psychopaths-business-leadership-csr/.

2 *lying in order to get what I want*: "Psychopathy Test," PsychCentral, November 18, 2020, psychcentral.com/quizzes/psychopathy-quiz.

4 *Ultimately, this enhances the bottom line*: Nancy Cooper, "America's Greatest Workplaces 2023," *Newsweek*, July 21, 2023, newsweek.com/rankings/americas-greatest-workplaces-2023.

7 *scientific research backs her up*: Priya J. Wickramaratne et al., "Social Connectedness as a Determinant of Mental Health: A Scoping Review," *PLOS ONE* 17, no. 10 (2022): e0275004, doi.org/10.1371/journal.pone.0275004.

The 7 Core Components of "You Belong Here"

30 *such as a racial minority*: *Merriam-Webster Online Dictionary*, "microaggression," merriam-webster.com/dictionary/microaggression.

30 *interrupt a woman than another man*: Kieran Snyder, "How to Get Ahead as a Woman in Tech: Interrupt Men," *Slate*, July 23, 2014, slate.com/human-interest/2014/07/study-men-interrupt-women-more-in-tech-workplaces-but-high-ranking-women-learn-to-interrupt.html.

30 *a universal phenomenon*: Susan Chira, "The Universal Phenomenon of Men Interrupting Women," *New York Times*, June 14, 2017, nytimes.com/2017/06/14/business/women-sexism-work-huffington-kamala-harris.html.

30 *workplace microaggressions she hears about*: Lydia Dishman, "How to Shut Down 'Microaggressions' at Work," *Fast Company*, March 7, 2017, fastcompany.com/3068670/how-to-shut-down-microagressions-at-work.

31 *ask you a question—instead*: Tanzina Vega, "Where Are You 'Really' From? Try Another Question," CNN, August 25, 2017, cnn.com/2017/06/20/opinions/where-are-you-really-from-vega-opinion/index.html.

2: Be the Keeper of the Safety Flame

34 *in his time plays many parts*: William Shakespeare, *As You Like It*, ed. Agnes Latham (London: Routledge, 1996), 2.7.139–142.

8 Proven Guidelines for Creating Belonging in a Hybrid Reality

46 *feel enthusiastic about the future:* Vibhas Ratanjee, "Successful Organizational Change Needs a Strong Narrative," Gallup, April 30, 2021, gallup.com/workplace/349295/successful-organizational-change-needs-strong-narrative.aspx.

46 *psychiatric patients treated in primary care:* Monica Vermani, Madalyn Marcus, and Martin A. Katzman, "Rates of Detection of Mood and Anxiety Disorders in Primary Care: A Descriptive, Cross-Sectional Study," *Primary Care Companion for CNS Disorders* 13, no. 2 (2011): PCC.10m01013, doi.org/10.4088/PCC.10m01013.

53 *You have a large malignant tumor:* Fred Reichheld, *Winning on Purpose: The Unbeatable Strategy of Loving Customers* (Boston: Harvard Business Review Press, 2021), xiii.

55 *it's your response, psychologists say*: Elizabeth Bernstein, "Have Better Conversations with Friends—or Anyone," *Wall Street Journal*, July 26, 2022, wsj.com/articles/have-better-conversations-with-friendsor-anyone-11658845993.

56 *that was a drawing card*: Jason Zinoman, "Review: Chris Rock's 'Selective Outrage' Strikes Back," *New York Times*, May 5, 2023, nytimes.com/2023/03/05/arts/television/chris-rock-netflix.html.

4: Change Your Rules for Relatedness

67 *access to new information and opportunities*: Katie Terrell Hanna and Ivy Wigmore, "Weak Tie Theory," TechTarget, January 2023, techtarget.com/whatis/definition/weak-tie-theory.

69 *40 percent of Americans live by themselves*: Richard Fry and Kim Parker, "Rising Share of U.S. Adults Are Living without a Spouse or Partner," Pew Research Center, October 5, 2021, pewresearch.org/social-trends/2021/10/05/rising-share-of-u-s-adults-are-living-without-a-spouse-or-partner/.

69 *30 percent of Canadians live alone*: Statistics Canada, "Home Alone: More Persons Living Solo Than Ever Before, but Roomies the Fastest Growing Household Type," *The Daily*, July 13, 2022, 150.statcan.gc.ca/n1/daily-quotidien/220713/dq220713a-eng.htm.

The 6 Rules for Relationship Health

72 *who can support me*: Dr. Diane McIntosh and Corey Hirsch, "Luke Prokop," *Blindsided* podcast, *The Player's Tribune*, December 1, 2022, theplayerstribune.com/posts/luke-prokop-nhl-hockey-nashville-predators-mental-health-blindsided-podcast.

75 *continuing longer than another person or thing*: *Merriam-Webster Online Dictionary*, "survival," merriam-webster.com/dictionary/survival.

80 *negative emotions in the relationship*: Kyle Benson, "The #1 Thing Couples Fight About," The Gottman Institute, gottman.com/blog/one-thing-couples-fight-about/.

82 *go above and beyond their job descriptions*: Rob Cross, Reb Rebele, and Adam Grant, "Collaborative Overload," *Harvard Business Review*, January–February 2016, hbr.org/2016/01/collaborative-overload.

6: Know That without the Yin, the Yang Will Crash and Burn

94 *typical male and female personality profiles*: Scott Barry Kaufman, "Taking Sex Differences in Personality Seriously," *Scientific American*, December 12, 2019, blogs.scientificamerican.com/beautiful-minds/taking-sex-differences-in-personality-seriously/.

94 *score higher on self-estimates of intelligence*: Sophie von Stumm, Tomas Chamorro-Premuzic, and Adrian Furnham, "Decomposing Self-Estimates of Intelligence: Structure and Sex Differences across 12 Nations," *British Journal of Psychology* 100, part 2 (May 2009): 429–442, doi.org/10.1348/000712608X357876.

94 *measured as an ability—are negligible*: Arthur R. Jensen, *The g Factor: The Science of Mental Ability* (Westport, CT: Praeger, 1998).

96 *industry average than all other firms*: Mekala Krishnan et al., "Ten Things to Know about Gender Equality," McKinsey Global Institute, September 21, 2020, mckinsey.com/featured-insights/diversity-and-inclusion/ten-things-to-know-about-gender-equality.

7: Accept That the Only Person You Can Control Is You

111 *the other person typically responds in kind*: Elizabeth Bernstein, "Have Better Conversations with Friends—or Anyone," *Wall Street Journal*, July 26, 2022, wsj.com/articles/have-better-conversations-with-friendsor-anyone-11658845993.

112 *highest for middle-aged white men*: American Foundation for Suicide Prevention, "Suicide Statistics," May 19, 2023, afsp.org/suicide-statistics/.

9: Keep Body and Soul Together

124 *consider their families dysfunctional*: Soulaima Gourani, "What Does Having a 'Real' Family Mean?" *Forbes*, November 24, 2019, forbes.com/sites/soulaimagourani/2019/11/24/what-does-having-a-real-family-mean/?sh=20829a5b1871.

127 *through enhanced chronic inflammation*: Yuna Koyama et al., "Interplay between Social Isolation and Loneliness and Chronic Systemic Inflammation during the COVID-19 Pandemic in Japan: Results from U-CORONA Study," *Brain, Behavior, and Immunity* 94 (May 2021): 51–59, doi.org/10.1016/j.bbi.2021.03.007.

128 *reduced hippocampal volume:* Bruno Lima Giacobbo et al., "Brain-Derived Neurotrophic Factor in Brain Disorders: Focus on Neuroinflammation," *Molecular Neurobiology* 56 (2019): 3295–312, doi.org/10.1007/s12035-018-1283-6.

128 *other psychiatric disorders*: Ronald S. Duman, Satoshi Deyama, and Manoela Viar Fogaça, "Role of BDNF in the Pathophysiology and Treatment of Depression: Activity-Dependent Effects Distinguish Rapid-Acting Antidepressants," *European Journal of Neuroscience* 53, no. 1 (2021): 126–39, doi.org/10.1111/ejn.14630; Eugenia Murawska-Ciałowicz et al., "BDNF Impact on Biological Markers of Depression—Role of Physical Exercise and Training," *International Journal of Environmental Research and Public Health* 18, no. 14 (2021): 7553, doi.org/10.3390/ijerph18147553.

10: Remake Your Memories to Enrich Your Future

132 *myself as hopelessly broken anymore*: Dr. Diane McIntosh, *This Is Depression: A Comprehensive, Compassionate Guide for Anyone Who Wants to Understand Depression* (Vancouver: Page Two, 2019), 47.

5 Ways to Create Your Own Predictability

149 *reasons for future outcomes by 30 percent*: Gary Klein, "Performing a Project Premortem," *Harvard Business Review*, September 2007, hbr.org/2007/09/performing-a-project-premortem.

12: Understand That Pressure Is the Price You Pay for Success

163 *they got up to bat, they did neither:* Ross Carey, "Your Average Hall of Famer," *Replacement Level* podcast, July 22, 2021, replacementlevelpodcast.com/2012/07/22/your-average-hall-of-famer/.

163 *average seventeen times an hour:* Kim Lephart, "Toddlers Weeble, Wobble and Fall Down—When Is It Cause for Concern?" Early Intervention Strategies for Success, January 9, 2014, veipd.org/earlyintervention/2014/01/09/toddlers-weeble-wobble-and-fall-down-when-is-it-cause-for-concern/.

163 *If someone says no, just say NEXT!*: Jack Canfield, Facebook, November 18, 2015, facebook.com/JackCanfieldFan/posts/10153285514315669.

13: Accept That Living on the Brink Is the Cost of Creating Breakthroughs

170 *had risen to 53 percent*: Ipsos, *CMA 2021 National Physician Health Survey*, August 24, 2022, cma.ca/sites/default/files/2022-08/NPHS_final_report_EN.pdf.

14: Recognize That Stress Attacks Us All—Even the Champions

179 *experience, resilience, and perseverance*: Dr. Diane McIntosh and Corey Hirsch, "Kevin Love," *Blindsided* podcast, *The Player's Tribune* January 19, 2022, theplayerstribune.com/posts/keving-love-cleveland-cavs-nba-basketball-mental-health-blindsided-podcast.

181 *baseline of 36.4 percent just months before*: Anjel Vahratian, Stephen J. Blumberg, Emily P. Terlizzi, and Jeannine S. Schiller, "Symptoms of Anxiety or Depressive Disorder and Use of Mental Health Care among Adults during the COVID-19 Pandemic—United States, August 2020–February 2021," *Morbidity and Mortality Weekly Report* 70, no. 13 (2021): 490–94, doi.org/10.15585/mmwr.mm7013e2.

16: Know That Trust Is the Most Valuable Thing You Can Give

195 *over fifty—by a wide margin*: Aidan Connaughton, "Social Trust in Advanced Economies Is Lower among Young People and Those with Less Education," Pew Research Center, December 3, 2020, pewresearch.org/fact-tank/2020/12/03/social-trust-in-advanced-economies-is-lower-among-young-people-and-those-with-less-education/.

18: Understand That Resilience Can Be Reproduced

219 *I'm responsible for telling them*: WD-40 Company, "Maniac Pledge: We Nurture a Culture of Accountability," wd40company.com/our-tribe/tribal-culture/#maniac-pledge.

19: Build on Your Maturity Factor: Be Intentional

226 *when they smell cigarette smoke*: "Know Your Brain: Nucleus Accumbens," Neuroscientifically Challenged, neuroscientificallychallenged.com/posts/know-your-brain-nucleus-accumbens.

7 Steps to Building the Future

235 *Let's make it better:* Esther Bintliff, "Positive Feedback: The Science of Criticism That Actually Works," *Financial Times*, July 21, 2022, ft.com/content/a681ac3c-73b8-459b-843c-0d796f15020e.

21: Know That the Ultimate Safety Zone Is Courageous Creativity

250 *what is conveniently on hand*: *Merriam-Webster Online Dictionary*, "MacGyver," merriam-webster.com/dictionary/MacGyver.

Epilogue: Become the Safe-Haven-Recharging-Station

259 *HR leaders in North America today*: SHRM, *2022–2023 SHRM State of the Workplace Report*, shrm.org/hr-today/trends-and-forecasting/research-and-surveys/Documents/2022-2023%20State%20of%20the%20Workplace%20Report.pdf.

259 *even further costs in the long run*: Jim Harter, "U.S. Employee Engagement Needs a Rebound in 2023," Gallup, January 25, 2023, gallup.com/workplace/468233/employee-engagement-needs-rebound-2023.aspx.

260 *team that wins with its customers*: Fred Reichheld, *Winning on Purpose: The Unbeatable Strategy of Loving Customers* (Boston: Harvard Business Review Press, 2021), 73.

PHOTO: JOHN CARVALHO

PHOTO: JAMIE-LEE FUOCO

About the Authors

MIKE LIPKIN is president of Environics/Lipkin, a global research and motivation company based in Toronto. He is also an international strategic coach, guide, and potentiator to high performers everywhere. He combines his personal experience of talking to a million people in sixty-seven countries with his rigorous research on extraordinary performance to create breakthroughs with others by any legal means possible.

Mike was raised in Johannesburg, South Africa. He immigrated to Toronto, Canada, in 2001 where he now lives with his wife, Hilary, and their two dogs. This is Mike's ninth book.

A RESPECTED PSYCHIATRIST, author, and educator, Dr. Diane McIntosh is a passionate advocate for better mental health care and a tireless champion for Canadians suffering from mental health challenges. Diane believes every Canadian deserves the best mental health care possible so that they can live full lives of physical and mental well-being.

Throughout her career, Diane has worked to raise the profile of mental health issues in Canada and around the world. She's established medical education and advocacy programs, published numerous blogs and op-eds, and lectures widely on mental health issues.

A key theme in Diane's advocacy is the urgent need to improve the quality of care and treatment options available for people diagnosed with mental illness. The severe toll COVID has taken on Canadians' mental health has brought these important issues into even sharper focus. Diane believes that mental health is health and that improving the accuracy of psychiatric diagnoses of mental health issues is key to early intervention and successful treatment.

Diane also co-hosts *Blindsided*, an award-winning podcast exploring mental health issues, with former NHL goalie Corey Hirsch. She's also the host of the podcast *Wicked Mind*, where she explores issues related to access to mental health care. Her most recent book, *This Is Depression*, is an Amazon Canada bestseller.

Let's Start a Conversation

LET'S TALK ABOUT how Diane and I can help you and your team become icons of belonging through our customized live keynotes, seminars, and workshops.

mikelipkin.com
mike.lipkin@environics.ca
1 416 969 2822
1 416 917 6007 cell

@MikeLipkin
facebook.com/MikeLipkinMotivation/
linkedin.com/in/mikelipkin